T0078052

One Hundred Saris and Servants Galore

My Life in Lahore

Lillian Greene

authorHOUSE·

AuthorHouse™ UK
1663 Liberty Drive
Bloomington, IN 47403 USA
www.authorhouse.co.uk
Phone: UK TFN: 0800 0148641 (Toll Free inside the UK)
         UK Local: (02) 0369 56322 (+44 20 3695 6322 from outside the UK)

Published by AuthorHouse 12/14/2021

ISBN: 978-1-6655-9480-6 (sc)
ISBN: 978-1-6655-9479-0 (e)

For my children

Contents

A Final Farewell

December 1969, the day of our departure. And it was raining. Nothing unusual about that. Raining, I mean. Cheshire would not be the lush county it is without the bountiful rainfall that blesses its hills and vales.

A brief, refreshing downpour would have been more welcome but this was the typical, endless drizzle, that clung like miserable parasites to all and sundry, damping the ambience and the most cheerful of souls.

Not mine, though. Not today! A zany cocktail of emotion, positivity, and elation flowing through my veins, I was about to embark on the greatest adventure of my life; one I could never have imagined, not even in my wildest dreams. But Mustafa had made up his mind. We were leaving our home to travel thousands of miles across the world to his homeland – Pakistan.

The decision to uproot our lives was not the outcome of a facetious or impulsive whim. In a way, it was thrust upon us. By nature, Mustafa was calm and level-headed. He had established himself in his profession as a computer development engineer, part of an elite team working in competition with IBM on the development of new computer systems. In our neighbourhood, he was considered affluent. Owning a three-bedroom house and Triumph Herald estate car, and the only car in our road, spoke volumes of a person's social standing in those days.

But here we were, about to leave all that behind and begin a new life in an under-developed country where so many uncertainties and few opportunities awaited us, and where Mustafa stood little chance of securing a job as a computer engineer. Why then this sudden decision to up all and move to Pakistan?

It was his father who had encouraged him to pursue higher studies in electrical engineering. Facilitated it, too. He had literally worked day and night, running a shop during the day, and working a night shift on the railways to pay for Mustafa's college fees and other expenses. Now in his mid-sixties, he had recently been diagnosed with a serious heart condition and the prognosis was not good. Heart surgery in the 1960s was in its infancy in the UK and virtually unheard of in Pakistan.

For several days after receiving the letter from his elder brother, *Bhai Jan* as he called him, telling him about his father's failing health, urging him to return to Pakistan, Mustafa seemed somewhat disturbed, whereas I was full of enthusiasm. The move would be good for all of us, I persuaded. His father had often expressed his desire to see us, as well as his concerns for the children's upbringing, repeatedly questioning how we planned to raise our children as Muslims in a non-Muslim land where even Christianity was suffering a serious decline, and churches, once full every Sunday, stood vacant and virtually abandoned.

Bubbles had started primary school, and Jimmy went to playschool three times a week. They were growing up so fast. But how would I be able to compete in a new world disorder where religion was being cast by the wayside? How could I educate my children to be practicing Muslims when I was myself a convert and a novice? Moving to Pakistan was surely the answer to all our problems.

So, the decision was final, and for the past couple of weeks we had been racing around like crazy, often with children in tow, trying to pack all we could for our life ahead. Easier said than done! What to take and what to leave behind? The stark reality began to penetrate that we were about to leave behind a way of life we were all accustomed to living.

Bubbles, so nicknamed because she had an effervescent personality and infectious giggle, had said her goodbyes to her teacher and school friends. She had also gone to the farm at the end of the lane to bid farewell to the ponies and her dream of ever having a pony of her own, which is what we had promised her.

"Don't worry!" Mustafa had assured her. "There are lots of ponies in Pakistan. In Lahore especially the streets are full of them. Well, not exactly ponies. Donkeys! But same thing, really. Once we've settled down, I promise I'll buy one for you." A promise that made her jump for joy and gave her something to look forward to.

The thought of leaving the depressing dampness of Cheshire behind for warmer climes the other side of the world had certainly bolstered the move. Still, it was not easy, leaving and saying goodbye. Our little house on the hill, now sold, had been our home for the past six years and had witnessed the birth of our four children, Bubbles, Jimmy, Beenish, and Biba, all pet names.

Of course, they had proper names as well. Muslim names with beautiful meanings, carefully chosen by his parents, but Mustafa preferred to call them by pet names, which was a common practice in his family, it seems, and I saw no reason to oppose it.

Our neighbours had been our only friends, though not intimate due to varied lifestyles. We did not drink alcohol, which meant no clubbing and pubbing. Every Saturday, Mustafa played bridge with a group of colleagues, but unlike them he never drank alcohol. Once a month, he would drive to London to buy *halal meat*, meat from animals slaughtered the Islamic way. Any meat that was not halal, and pork in particular, were totally off the menu.

Our children often played with other children in our road, and our immediate neighbour, Ruth, who had two children of her own, would always invite ours to play in her front garden when the weather was fine. Her son was older than Jimmy and just learning to walk, whereas Jimmy could race across her lawn, dribbling a large football, which never ceased to amaze her.

A jewel of a person, Ruth was my closest friend, and someone I knew I could depend on in time of need. She was at my bedside when our third child, little Beenish, was born. Labour pains started early in the morning, and later that day I had an antenatal check-up. I honestly didn't think I would be able to keep the appointment, but I did. Mustafa couldn't take me. He was at work. So, I waddled down the hill to the bus stop and waited a good half hour for the bus that would drop me off at the local surgery.

Waiting to be seen, I had to hold my breath several times, silently bearing contractions. I was certain the baby was on its way, but the doctor casually dismissed the thought. Braxton Hicks contractions, she assured me, not unusual towards the end of pregnancy. So, clasping my precious bulge as heavily pregnant women intuitively do, I left the surgery and took the bus home.

By evening the pains were coming quick and strong, so Mustafa, panic now written all over his face, rang the midwife. I could hear her voice, slow, deliberately calming and composed. She assured him there was still plenty of time, probably several hours. Ring me when the pains are five minutes apart. And she hung up.

Plenty of time! How did she know? I wanted to scream at her, "The baby's coming!" but an excruciating contraction prevented me. The pains were now so strong with very short intervals in between. Mustafa made another urgent call to the midwife. This time she told him she would soon be on her way.

Now *I* was beginning to panic. What if she didn't arrive in time? I called out to Mustafa who had gone downstairs to play with the children, to distract them while I coped with the ever-increasing contractions, snorting like a horse to help stem the urge to scream.

Mustafa stood nervously in the doorway, afraid of what I might say. "You might have to deliver this baby," I said, breathing heavily through a mighty contraction.

Mustafa's jaw dropped and he stared at me with shifting emotions, mostly fear. "What about Ruth!" he blurted. "Let's call Ruth." And his face suddenly relaxed as though a mountain had been lifted from his shoulders.

Poor Ruth! She too looked shocked when I told her she might have to deliver the baby. "I'm sorry, Ruth, and please don't mind, but I breathe heavily like a cart horse when the pains come. It stops me from screaming." A massive contraction followed, and I gave the best demonstration of snorting imaginable.

The contraction was barely over when the midwife finally arrived. A quick examination and she reeled backwards. "Oh, my goodness!" she said, hurriedly throwing off her overcoat. "Baby's crowning. You're about to deliver."

She was lucky. I wanted to say, "I told you so!" but before I could utter a word, a sudden urge to push took over, and moments later little Beenish was born. I waited anxiously to hear her cry, but she didn't. So, I eased myself up to look at her.

"She's got her thumb in her mouth," the midwife explained. "She's probably been sucking it in the womb. Some babies do that."

She took the thumb out and I heard what all mothers want to hear, the new-born's first cry. Moments later, she was quiet again, her tiny thumb back in her mouth. Great, I thought! She will be an easy baby to look after. And she was.

That was over two years ago. Our family had since grown. Little Biba, this year's addition, was now eight months old. Hers, on doctor's advice, had been a hospital delivery. Although my home deliveries had been straightforward, she said the risk of complications with a fourth delivery were significantly higher. So, while Ruth minded the children, Mustafa drove me to the hospital and then left.

I was given a sedative, so slept through most of the pains. But come morning, the pains jolted me into wakefulness. Attended to by a beautiful African nurse, I was delivered of our third baby girl.

I expected to be discharged the same day, but due to some minor concerns I was advised to stay for at least another day. But then Mustafa came with the children. Since they were not allowed in the wards, he brought them to the window. Bubbles and Jimmy waved excitedly, but little Beenish looked so vacant, so lost and forlorn. Her big blue eyes as wide as saucers, she just stared at me, perhaps wondering why I was lying in a big white bed with strangers all around.

And when Mustafa told me she had been calling out and searching for me in all the rooms of the house, I could not stay a moment longer.

The day of our departure, and we were packed and prepared for the long journey ahead. And while the children sat quietly on the sofa, Biba slept soundly in her carrycot. In the hallway, neatly lined against the staircase, was our luggage, confirmation that we were indeed ready to leave. Waiting, rather anxiously now, for Mustafa's friend, Mohammad, to arrive from London. He was going to accompany us to the airport and later return to clear the house of the things we had to leave behind, and then hand the keys over to the new owners.

Mustafa and Mohammad had been friends since early childhood. They attended the same primary and secondary schools. They even ended up together in college and university but with different choice of subjects. And when Mohammad came to England to study, Mustafa followed.

During one phase of their student life in Pakistan, their friendship met with plausible disapproval from their mothers. Mohammad's home was not far from the college, but Mustafa's was. So, at the end of every day, Mohammad would laugh and say, "*Yaar* (friend), I can't let you walk all that way alone," and would insist on accompanying him.

When they arrived at Mustafa's house, however, after a few minutes chit chat on the doorstep, Mustafa would say, "Yaar,

I can't let you walk all that way alone," and the two would be off again, this time back to Mohammad's house.

It was a serious matter for them, having to part, and they often ended up walking four or five times to one another's homes without entering. And invariably, when either mother saw her son on the doorstep, she would put the *tawa* (griddle) on the fire to make *chapatis* for him, only to take it off again when she saw he was gone; rather like the nursery rhyme, Polly put the kettle on, we'll all have tea. Suzy take it off again, they've all gone away.

Exasperated by these odd comings and goings, Mohammad's mother, a tall, imposing figure, was usually the one to put an end to their shenanigans with a good telling off, rolling pin in hand, poised for action. A great weapon and effective deterrent!

But those were days of carefree youth and romanticism, when Indian films were the most popular form of entertainment, films that greatly influenced the minds of the young movie goers. The melodramatic theme of most films was undying love. Mohammad and Mustafa wanted theirs to be a story of everlasting friendship.

A few years after our marriage, having enrolled for a course in neighbouring Lancashire, Mohammad came to live with us for almost a year. As always, he was great company and the children simply adored him. It also gave me the opportunity to discover a different side of him. He often played the magician, enthralling the children by making small things disappear. And unlike Mustafa and me, placid and slow plodding like carthorses, Mohammad was like a racehorse with superfast metabolism and a voracious appetite to match. He could get extremely irritable when hungry, so I had to be careful about serving meals on time. Once, while waiting for dinner, which was later than usual, he ate a whole loaf of sliced bread with butter!

⸺◆⸺

The doorbell rang and Mustafa rushed to answer it. Mohammad, at last! It must be. But no! It was Vera from across the road. She had bought our Hotpoint twin tub washing machine but had forgotten my instructions on how to use it. Could I possibly spare a few minutes to explain it all again, she wondered?

Well, apart from waiting for Mohammad I had nothing to do, so I agreed. "Stay sitting nicely," I told the children as I donned my coat and followed Vera to her home.

I was not away long. About ten to fifteen minutes, maybe, but when I returned the children were no longer on the sofa. Beenish was sitting at the top of the stairs, her favourite place, hugging the giant panda we had already decided was too big to take with us and had hidden away. Bubbles was dancing, twirling like a ballerina, and Jimmy was sitting on his pedal tractor, another toy we regretfully had to leave behind, making engine noises, pretending to drive. And small wonder that little Biba was awake, trying to sit herself up so she could watch the antics of her siblings.

"Oh, Mustafa! What happened?" I complained. "And how did they get these toys? I hid them so they wouldn't get upset again."

Before he could answer, the doorbell rang again. This time, it was Mohammad. At last, I sighed!

"You're late!" said Mustafa, giving his friend a hug and forgiving him before he had time to answer.

"Well, you know me," Mohammad replied in his jovial manner, eyes twinkly impishly and lips parting in a winsome smile that always ensured clemency. "I took a couple of wrong turns getting out of London."

While the children rushed to meet him, I quietly put the panda and tractor back in the under-stair cupboard, hoping that in the excitement of the moment they would now be forgotten. We were running late, so what followed was a hectic rush to get everyone and everything we needed into the car, lock up and leave. A last-minute check of tickets and passports and we were off.

As we drove down the steep hill, I looked back at our home. It was just a house now. Someone else's home-to-be. And all too soon it was out of sight. Determined to hold back the tears, I focussed on the journey ahead, praying it would be trouble-free, especially for the children who had never travelled beyond our hometown.

We arrived at Manchester airport only to hear an urgent announcement over the public address system. "Last call for Mustafa Mir and family! Mr Mustafa Mir, please go to gate number…"

Panic! Which gate did they say? Which way? And then, like a knight in shining armour, a Pakistan International Airline officer came to the rescue. "Mustafa Mir?" he asked.

"Yes, yes!" Mustafa replied, his eyes bulging like a petrified deer. I noticed Mohammad had a similar expression, nervous and wide-eyed, but I suspect his was due to guilt for making us late.

"Come!" said the officer, taking hold of Bubbles and Jimmy's hands and leading the way, while I held Biba and Mustafa carried Beenish. We walked and half-ran as fast as we could, turning a couple of times to look back and wave at Mohammad.

Finally, we reached the tarmac where the plane's propellers were revving, booming excitedly, eager to take to the sky. Moments later, we were in the air, on our way to London airport, the first leg of our epic, life-changing journey.

Having never flown before, I was unprepared for the dips as the plane gained height, and my stomach leapt to my throat for fear we were falling. But once we reached cruising height, it was so smooth it was difficult to imagine we were moving at all.

The children were sitting quietly, overtired probably, and overcome with the strangeness of it all. But then, they were always exceptionally well-behaved outside the home. Not inside! But outside good behaviour was always guaranteed, quite the opposite to other parents' experiences, I learned.

Every Saturday, we would walk to town to window-shop, and buy fruit and vegetables from the open market, and the children never misbehaved. Even hyperactive Jimmy, always a handful, would be on his best behaviour, except that he would tug persistently at Mustafa's sleeve, shouting, "Grabees, Daddy! Buy grabees!" *Grabees* being his word for grapes, his favourite fruit.

At home, Biba was a happy, trouble-free baby. Beenish was no trouble either, but contrary to her slight form she could be very loud when she wanted to be. Her favourite game was to sit on the top step of the stairs, an open story book resting on her knees, shouting out gibberish, interrupted with bouts of giggling, as though she was reading a funny story to an invisible audience below.

With Bubbles and Jimmy, however, it was a very different matter. They were the boisterous ones. One minute they would be playing together happily, moments later they would be locked in mortal combat, screaming, and pulling one another's hair. But whatever the reasons for their disagreements, they were always short-lived, and they would be the best of friends again in no time. And whenever I separated them, they would cry to be together again, so I learnt it was often better to let them sort out their own squabbles.

After a brief stopover at London airport, we were finally aboard the Boeing 707 that would take us to Karachi,

Pakistan. With the long, uninterrupted journey ahead, we could now relax and enjoy the flight. The children soon fell asleep in their seats, and while keeping an eye on them, Mustafa was reading through the daily newspapers. Biba had been fed and was sleeping peacefully in the bassinette, so I reclined my seat, closed my eyes, and gave way to the fatigue I had been fighting since we left home.

It was the exciting jet age, and as our plane zoomed ahead at an average cruising speed of over 500 knots per hour, my mind slowly drifted backwards in time.

Last of the Happy Kids

Standing on tiptoes beside her wicker crib, I was just able to put my head inside the hood and kiss my sister's plump, pink cheeks. I then rested my cheek against hers. I thought the smell of her delicate skin was simply divine, and it was so soft. Softer than anything else I knew. The smooth softness only new-born babies possess.

I kissed her again, but this time she woke up from her peaceful sleep and began to cry, her tiny lips trembling, and little arms and legs kicking and punching the air. I wanted to cuddle her but could not reach far enough, so I gently patted her, hoping she would stop crying and go back to sleep; and that's when Mum came and gently lifted her out of the crib.

"She's hungry. It's time for her feed," she said.

And that was my earliest recollection of childhood. A childhood filled with countless, wonderful memories!

Like all the other houses in the street, ours was a large, three-story semi. Not as grand as the detached houses on the other side of the main road that had four stories as well as a basement, a front garden with two double gates and a semi-circular driveway for horse-drawn carriages to enter one way and exit the other. Not that carriages were still around when I was a child. Those times had gone. For the privileged few, cars had taken over. There were trains, trams, and buses too, as well as horse-driven carts of all descriptions.

Still, ours was a lovely house. There was a small front garden with a shady tree, privet hedges enclosing a small lawn, and a variety of flowers bordering the pathway leading from the latched wooden gate to the big front door. But the back garden was our pride and joy, and a very different spectacle altogether. It was generous and purposeful with all manner of fruit and flora. Its two distinct halves were divided by a pathway of crazy paving slabs stretching all the way down the middle to a gate at the end.

The left side of the garden boasted a Lilac Tree, rose bushes, lupins, and other perennials, as well as a greenhouse for growing tomatoes. But Dad really went to town on the right side, which was most definitely his domain, probably inspired by the slogan *Dig for Victory* that encouraged everyone to grow their own food.

Due the war, there was a shortage of farm workers, many having enlisted in the armed forces, and an ever-increasing need for food to supply the troops, as well as the families of those who stayed behind to keep the home fires burning. And in 1940, the government introduced Food Rationing to ensure the fair distribution of all food and commodities.

It began with items such as butter, sugar, and meat, and eventually included most foods, except for fruit and vegetables. Everyone in Britain was issued a ration book they registered with a shop of their choice, and each time they purchased something, the shopkeeper would cross off the relevant coupon in the ration book. It was a simple but brilliant system that lasted fourteen years and ensured everybody had a fair share of the food available.

When I started school, sweets were still on ration. But I remember as if it were yesterday the jubilation when sweet rationing finally ended. It was February 1953, and did we indulge! Liquorice sticks, dolly mixture, blackjacks, lemon sherbets and gob-stoppers – as much as our pennies could buy! Something I blame for my poor teeth because thereafter we ate sweets almost every day, the sweet shop being the first place we went to after school and brushing teeth all too often overlooked.

Back to our garden, Dad's working side of it. Having served in the Royal Air Force during the war and being more of an intellectual with ambitions to enter the political arena, Dad exhibited exceptional talent and ingenuity when he turned his hand to gardening, and carpentry. Alongside the fence between our garden and our next-door neighbour's, he built a chicken run with an external, hinge-lid nest box that allowed us to collect the eggs easily.

Growing close to the kitchen window, was a huge cluster of rhubarb, tended mostly by Mum who kept it well fertilized with horse manure. Whenever the coalman, milkman or rag-and-bone man passed by our house she would go to the window to see if their horse had dropped any dung. If it had, off she would go, shovel in hand, to scoop it up.

Racing through the house with it, shouting, "Open the door! Open it!" she would dump it on the budding rhubarb. Strange, it occurs to me now, that even knowing how and why our rhubarb grew so well, we always loved eating it, whether it was with a sponge topping or in a delicious tart served with hot custard, or even raw, plucked fresh from the ground.

Then came the strawberries, and the blackcurrants, and redcurrants. There were a few gooseberry bushes too, all handy snacks when we were playing outside, although I think I was the only one who liked gooseberries, the plump, yellowy ripe ones. Until one evening that is, when we were all huddled in front of the coal fire, someone asked Mum where we came from. When it was my turn, she said she found me under a gooseberry bush.

Now, Mum's should be careful what they tell their children. From then onwards, I went off gooseberries, fruit I had always enjoyed, eaten freshly plucked from the bush or in a tasty, crusty pie. And the idea of being found "under" as opposed to "on" something, instilled in my childish mind a troubled sense of inferiority. Moreover, her answer only increased my curiosity and raised even more questions. How did she find me? Why was I there in the first place? And who put me there?

Back to the garden again!

We could have supplied a greengrocer's shop with all the vegetables our garden produced. There were onions, carrots, cabbages, cauliflowers, and turnips. Peas and runner beans supported by strings on tall wooden frames. We also had lettuces and radishes, and more besides.

Beyond this copious vegetable patch, at the very end of our garden, was a tool shed that we used as a den on rainy or wintry days. But despite the size and interesting diversity of our garden and the alluring shed, our favourite place lay outside our garden gate.

Although the war was over, evidence of it was literally on our doorstep. Just across the road, lay the ruins of a bombed-out house, and on the corner, the ghostly remains of a church. Stark reminders of the blitz, the German bombing campaign against Britain.

At the onset of World War II, our family, excluding Dad who was serving in the Royal Air Force, moved to Mum's ancestral home in the Wiltshire countryside, a chocolate-box thatched cottage, and the place where I was born. Only when the war was over did we return to the house in the London suburbs.

The houses in our area were built in such a way, there was a quadrangle between the back gardens of our street and those of the street behind, and still occupying that space were two communal air raid shelters, testament to that dreadful summer of 1940 when for fifty-seven consecutive nights the German Luftwaffe dropped their deadly bombs on London and other English cities.

Being so young, we had never experienced the sound of sirens – a wailing, spine-chilling warning that German fighter planes loaded with deadly bombs, or the dreaded doodlebugs, cruise missiles also known as buzz bombs, were on their way. Nor had we witnessed the terror and panic as people, old and young, with toddlers, new-born, and even unborn babies, abandoned their homes and raced to the safety of the shelters.

There were times when the bombing lasted all night, when leaving the shelter was suicide. While some huddled together on the concrete floor, others tried to get some sleep on the wooden bunk beds that lined the walls. And there were times when people sang to boost morale and drown the dreadful sounds above.

For us though, the shelters held much happier memories. They were our playground, our special domain. A place of fun and laughter where we spent most of our playtime hours, and where nearly all our outside games and capers took place.

Like free-range chickens, we were allowed out each day to roam, weather permitting, and ushered back in the afternoon for tea and later bed. And on warm summer days, all the children from our street would come flocking to the shelter area to play and explore.

Girls would turn up with five-stones, skipping ropes and hula hoops, and the boys with guns, bows and arrows, bats and balls, their pockets often bursting with marbles. But whatever games we played, there was no gender disparity, so most of the time we played together.

Tip-it-and-run was one of our favourite pastimes, a simple game involving a cricket bat and ball, a bowler, batsman and fielders. The rules were simple, although we often bent them or cheated, and arguing over whether we were out or not was always part of the fun.

If we hit the ball, we had to run to the other end, and if we made it safely to the marked line before someone hit it with the ball, we scored a run. But if a fielder hit the line with the ball before we reached it, we were out, and the next player was in. The one with the highest number of runs at the end of play was the winner. Looking back though, winning was never a big part of any of our games. It was more about having fun together.

Another favourite game was Tin Can Tommy, which required a ball, an empty tin can, and two sticks, each about six to eight inches long, not that we ever measured them. Usually, we used twigs and broke them to about the right size. We would then divide ourselves into two teams, players, and defenders.

One of us would place the tin, any empty can would do, upside down on the ground and lay two sticks, one crossed over the other, on top of it. The first player would stand on a marked spot, a few yards away from the tin, while the defenders would stand at a distance, waiting for him or her to throw the ball, the aim being to hit the can and knock the sticks off. If he failed to do so, the next player would take a turn, but if he succeeded, then all the members of his side would scramble to get the tin and sticks back in place, while the defenders would try to stop them by hitting a player with the ball. And whoever was hit, would be out of the game.

The defenders would try to get all the players out in this way, but if the playing side managed to restore the tin and sticks to their original position, they would shout, "Tin Can Tommy!" and would be declared the winners of that innings. Sounds complicated? It was actually very simple. Very noisy! But tremendous fun.

"It" was another common ball game we enjoyed. One person would be chosen to be "It", and while all the other players darted here and there trying to dodge him, "It" had to throw the ball and try to hit someone. If he succeeded, the person he hit would then become "It", and so the game went on. But if someone was hit while his feet were off the ground, he was spared from being "It".

If we saw the ball coming at us, we would try to leap into the air before it hit us or scramble onto anything, even someone's jacket or jumper if there happened to be one lying on the ground. I was always very good at that. We all were. Anything to avoid being out!

There was a time during those carefree days when we had a special air raid shelter gang. To become a member, we would have to pass an initiation ceremony, which involved eating a special sandwich – a slice of bread topped with melted candle grease. Folded over, it became a candle-grease sandwich. Of course, it was awful and almost impossible to swallow, so one bite was sufficient to qualify.

Holding lighted candles, we would occasionally venture inside the shelter, which was usually flooded with rainwater because the trapdoors in the roof were missing. We would go as far as the nearest bunks and then sit on a bench and chat for a while. It was dark, dank, and eerie at the best of times, but then something happened that spelt the end of our shelter gang for ever.

We were sitting on a bench, candles flickering and threatening to go out any minute, when suddenly there was a creepy, ghostly sound, followed by the appearance of a green-headed monster that scared the daylights out of us.

Screaming crazily, we ran out, the monster close on our heels. Outside, in the glaring daylight, we realised the monster was none other than our gang leader wearing a green gas mask. We often laughed about it afterwards, but we never ventured inside the shelter again.

Just as well! Inside, here was an eerie foreboding about them, as though all the horrors of the war were encapsulated in its dark, dank passageways. And if its walls could speak, they would tell more tales of sorrowful sighs and tearfulness than cheerful chatter.

Abandoning the shelter was not the end of our fun. Far from it! Close by, there was a huge, bombed site that had once been a grand, three-story house with a massive garden. Judging by the trees and flowers that survived the blitz, and despite a huge crater and mounds of rubble, the garden had evidently been a splendid one. The house, too! Once someone's home, it now stood like a forsaken ruin. Did the family survive the war, I often wondered? If so, where were they now?

Whatever had transpired, this land now belonged to us. It was part of our domain. Posing as both rider and steed, one hand in front holding the reins, the other behind, raised, and ready to pat our buttocks to stir us on, we would gallop over the wild terrain, stopping at intervals for our steed to whinny and rear up like the Lone Ranger's famous horse, Silver. At war with the red Indians hiding in the bushes with their home-made bows and arrows, we would fire our guns as we rode by, usually a closed fist with extended forefinger, recoiling with every shot.

The biggest boy in our neighbourhood became our self-elected leader and set up a tent that only his chosen posse could enter. Day after long, sunny day was spent in that forsaken garden that was now our wonderful Wild West.

The end of summer heralded our scrumping season. Nearly all the gardens behind the shelter had fruit trees with branches overhanging the fences or walls. The first problem was how to reach the fruit. The second was to avoid being caught. And the biggest dare of all was to pluck the plump, ripe pears from the witch's garden.

We all thought she was a witch because she was very old and wrinkly and always wore black. A long black, full-skirted dress, a black lace cap, and a black woollen shawl! The reason she wore black was because she was a widow, but we didn't know that then.

In our childish minds, only witches wore black. Her quaking voice as she shouted and waved her walking stick at us whenever she caught us near her garden wall indisputably certified her as a witch. The pears would only fall to the ground and rot if we did not pluck them, so we were not doing any harm, but being a witch, she disagreed.

On our legitimate patch there was a crab apple tree. The apples were too small and bitter to eat, so we used them as ammunition in another of our pastimes, a Crab Apple War, two sides trying to hit one another with the tiny apples.

***

Despite the hardships of post-war Britain, we were happy. Last of the happy kids! That's what we were. It was there, in the air and everywhere, the desire to be free, to have fun and to make every precious moment worthwhile.

Times were undoubtedly hard, and people often struggled to make ends meet. In our home, despite our bountiful garden produce and always having food on the table, there was strict observance of "waste not, want not", even when rationing was over.

There were times, painful to recall, when I deeply felt the pinch of poverty. We were a big family, and occasionally

Mum would send me to the neighbouring spinsters' house to sell something of hers so she could buy the extra food that was always needed. The two old spinsters were very kind, and I knew they only bought the things Mum offered them just to help us through our difficult days.

Those little errands had a profound effect on me. If they burdened me with shame, they also aroused deep feelings of empathy and compassion. I became extremely sensitive to the misery and pain so often associated with poverty. And I learned to be thrifty and forever thankful.

I hated the war, what I knew of it. People were still talking about the horrors and atrocities, the hardship and heartache. We would watch war films on our latest and prized possession, a television with such a small screen it had a magnifier over it to make the picture bigger.

It still sends a chill down my spine to see men wearing big boots. In the war films we saw there was invariably a Nazi soldier, saluting and clicking his boots together, a sound that became synonymous with war and all the trauma and tragedy associated with it. War, if there must be war, should only be army against army, not the bombing, persecution and killing of innocent men, women, and children, whatever their colour, race, or creed. That is what I believe.

It baffled me that a man could be a loving, caring family man one moment, and the next become an insensitive beast capable of committing the worst atrocities imaginable against other human beings, including women and children like his own. How? What is it that can transform a God-fearing man into a heartless monster?

<hr />

For us, winter had its own privation. If it was cold outside, it was cold indoors, too. No double-glazing or central heating in those days. Only coal fires, cardigans, jumpers, mufflers, and stone or rubber hot water bottles for our beds.

Still, life was good. The warmth we shared, sitting around a blazing coal fire, toasting roughly cut slices of crusty bread on a long fork, so wholesome and mouth-watering when buttered, hot from the coals. And the discourse that at times could become as heated as the fire.

On those wintry days, there was never any dearth of things to do, and although I cannot recall ever buying any, we had a treasure trove of toys. Puzzles, usually with several pieces missing, spinning tops and humming tops, marbles, dominoes, bagatelle, clockwork toys and a variety of board games; all from jumble sales. Mum once brought home a low pram without a hood, left over after the local church jumble sale. I could not understand why she thought we needed it.

"No one wanted it," Mum explained. "So, I thought it might be useful for bringing the weekly ration, but you can play with it if you like."

And play with it we did. We would take turns to sit in it and be pushed to the end of the road and back. Big as I was, squeezing into it and being pushed along was something indescribably satisfying. Only someone who has experienced it knows the feeling.

By far the best jumble sale bargain was an old typewriter. It had a double-coloured ribbon, black and red, but because the black part was so well-used the ink had dried out, which meant I could only type in red ink. But what did that matter? I would hammer away at the metal keys, typing adventure stories. I even typed a three-act play, a farcical comedy, but after that the red ink dried up and the typewriter had to be abandoned.

When I showed my English teacher the red-typed script of my play, he liked it so much, he asked me to present it on the school stage at the end of the winter term. And I did, earning much laughter and applause. And that was when I must have caught the writing bug.

<hr />

Winter was synonymous with Christmas and all the exciting activities leading up to it. Saving pennies for presents, buying and wrapping them, baking, decorating, and door-to-door Carol Singing.

In our home, it started with baking. Since Christmas pudding needed time to mature, Mum would make it well in advance, but we were not so enthusiastic about that, except to watch her pop the silver sixpence into the mix, a lucky surprise for the one who found it in their portion of pudding on Christmas Day.

When it came to making the cake, however, we would all stand around the kitchen table, helping, tasting, watching, and waiting, hoping to have the big wooden spoon to lick afterwards or the consolation of sharing the cake mixture left in the mixing bowl.

Mince pies were made on Christmas Eve, usually by my younger sister, the one whose velvety cheeks I could not resist kissing when she was a baby. With her big blue eyes, rosy cheeks, and thick, golden braids, she was a sight to behold, even with flour on her face and in her hair. And whilst I stood watching her, I remember feeling proud of how pretty she was. Hardworking, generous, and good-hearted, too. Making good use of the hoodless pram Mum brought home from the jumble sale, she would deliver the grocer's larger Christmas orders, earning enough money to buy presents for everyone.

I was not much help in the kitchen, but I like to think I was of some use when it came to the Christmas decorations. That, too, was a family affair with everyone doing their bit. Generally, decorating the Christmas tree was easy because we never had a very tall one. We did not have the space, for one thing, and Mum hated the mess the falling needles made. On the premise that a smaller tree made less mess, our tree was never more than four feet tall.

Decorating the house, on the other hand, could sometimes prove problematic, like stretching a roll of crepe paper streamer across the room, only to see it fall from your hand just as you were about to fix it to the wall. When fully decorated though, our house would be a riot of colour, with loops of homemade paperchains, twirling streamers crossing the room, bright red honeycomb paper bells hanging from the ceiling, and sprigs of holly everywhere.

Christmas was truly special in those days, when life was simple and little things meant so much, and when there was more love than presents to give and share.

How blissful those long summer days! No worries! No hurry! All the time in the world to make daisy chains or search for four-leafed clover. Lying on the grass, the damp, sweet-scented earth beneath our sun-warmed bodies, watching candyfloss clouds sail by in the bluest of skies, or eyes closed and minds drifting to a land of dreams.

Childhood summers were like no other. Sometimes, time stood still. Other times, it was so packed with adventure and excitement we lost all sense of time. Often, we would all go to our local park, which was just down the road, armed with a bottle of Tizer and packets of crisps with miniscule packets of salt inside.

There, we would sit on the grass, eagerly awaiting the arrival of the mobile cinema. The back of the van would lift to reveal a screen and we would be entertained with a variety of films. Charlie Chaplin, Laurel and Hardy, Tom and Jerry, and cowboy films, to name a few.

On warm, summer days, our front and back doors were always wide-open. The baby of our family would be left in his pram in the garden, to play or sleep as he pleased. Mothers would even leave their babies in their prams outside the shops while they went inside. And we had freedom to roam all day, so long as we were back home for tea.

Cats and dogs had freedom, too. Over the years, we had lots of pets. A large Alsatian cross, a tortoise, cats of various descriptions, budgerigars, guinea pigs and pigeons. My favourite pigeon was a soft, creamy brown tumbler that could somersault in the air as she flew.

No cars! No pick and drop service in those days! There were trains, of course, as well as trams and buses. But most of the time, we used Shank's pony. Sometimes, we would "follow the leader" and trek single file along the banks of the River Quaggy, armed with nets and empty jam jars for catching tiddlers like minnows or sticklebacks. And during the tadpole season, we would be out searching the local ponds for frogspawn.

We were a harmonious bunch. We shared the same enthusiasm to enjoy and explore, and in our domain each one of us was king or queen. A regular excursion took us across Black Heath to Greenwich Park, on the banks of the River Thames. With its ancient royal palace, it was once the popular residence of many kings and queens, and the birthplace and playground of Henry VIII. It was our playground, too, where all sorts of amusement awaited us.

We could watch the miniature boats on the small pond on the heath or go down to the river and watch the real boats go by. And there was a bigger pond inside the park with pedal-boat rides. In between, the deer enclosure, Plum Pudding Hill, the Royal Observatory, and the all-important line that separates east from west and by which world time is calculated – the Prime Meridian.

Once, we were playing near the boating pond when one of us decided to walk along the edge of the low wall enclosing the pond. If that was not crazy enough, someone then suggested (I hope it wasn't me) that we dip one foot into the water as we walked. I can hear it now, someone saying, "Step, step, dip! Step, step, dip!" as we walked single file along the narrow wall, holding onto the one in front.

And then the unthinkable but inevitable happened. One of us lost their footing, fell into the pond, and disappeared beneath the murky water. It was our little sister, the one I kissed when she was asleep in her crib. Before we could even think what to do, a dashing young man in his air force uniform rushed forward and pulled her out. Cradling her sodden, shivering body in his arms, he turned to us and said, "Follow me! My house is nearby." So, we followed, scared that our little sister might die. And all because of someone's scatterbrain idea!

His house was indeed close by. Calling out to his mother to come quickly, he rushed straight through to the kitchen, and without asking permission to enter, we followed. His mother quickly removed all her clothes and gave her a warm bath in the kitchen sink. After wrapping her in a large towel, she gave her a drink of hot cocoa and then dressed her in one of her own blouses, which of course was far too big. We all enjoyed a cup of hot cocoa that day. It warmed us and helped to cheer us up after our dreadful ordeal.

Cradling our little sister in his arms once more, the gallant young soldier followed us all the way to our home. And although I remember this incident vividly, I cannot recall Mum's reaction when a stranger, carrying her little girl, arrived at her doorstep.

———⊷✦⊶———

Trips to Greenwich park and Blackheath were a regular thing. Once, we happened to be standing by the river, looking across the water, when our big sister asked, "Who wants to go to the other side?"

Beckoning us to follow her, she then raced off, and like faithful minions we followed. We entered a circular, hut-like building with red-bricked walls and a blue, glazed dome, and just inside was a spiral flight of stairs, long and steep, and seemingly endless. The loud clickety-click of our shoes as we descended scared the daylights out of me, spurring me on faster, terrifying me even more as though some gory monster was close behind us. The last step, a left turn, and the long, semi-circular tunnel stood before us.

We had already noticed the water dribbling down the white, tiled walls, so when our big sister shouted, "Come on! Run before the roof caves in!" we ran for our lives, our screams echoing through the tunnel, fearful that at any moment the River Thames would come crashing down on us. They say, it takes about ten minutes to walk through the tunnel. We must have crossed it in half the time.

At the other end was another flight of stairs like those we descended on entering, but these we had to climb up, which seemed to take forever. Out in the open air, in the Island Gardens of the Isle of Dogs, my pounding heart settled to a steady rhythm, and I could breathe normally again.

But not for long. I remember emphatically saying to my sister, "I'll never, ever, go into that tunnel again," and her nonchalant reply, "But you'll have to, if you want to go back home. Unless you want to swim across the river."

The Greenwich foot tunnel was undeniably a feat of ingenuity, designed to allow people living on the south side of the River Thames easy access to the London shipyards and docks on the north side. For me, however, it was a scary place, and I never went there again.

The Best Days

They say schooldays are the best days of your life, but I would put a question mark on that statement. Not that I was unhappy at school, quite the contrary, but I did encounter problems, mainly because I was a scatterbrain and incorrigible giggler. It did not help that the girl I shared a desk with had a similar disposition. Pretty, with plump, rosy cheeks and beautiful ringlets, she was the picture of innocence. In truth, she was wickedly witty, and never failed to make me laugh.

During one lesson, Teacher was explaining plant regrowth, about how new shoots or branches grow to replace any that are broken or cut off. Chuckling to herself, she hurriedly drew something on a piece of paper and pushed it over to my side for me to see. It was a drawing of a man with a proper leg on his left side and a tiny new leg sprouting from the right side.

That did it! I put both hands over my mouth to muffle the sound of my giggling, and just when I thought I had things under control, she drew my attention to the drawing again. Whenever I calmed down, she showed me the drawing, which set me off once more. Gigglers once triggered lose control and everything is hilarious. Finally, our teacher had had enough, and I was made to stand outside in the assembly hall.

That should have had a sobering effect on me, but not so. Instead of standing quietly, feeling ashamed and repentant, I stood on the wooden bench set against the classroom wall and peered through the window into my classroom. When several classmates caught sight of me and smiled, I started to make silly faces to amuse them, bobbing out of sight whenever the class teacher looked my way. But then I mistimed a dodge and she caught me.

To say she was cross is an understatement. She dragged me back into the classroom and gave me a sound telling off, followed by a whack on each hand with a ruler, which put an end to my shenanigans, for a while at least. And she had the wisdom to change my seat so that my partner in crime and I were too far apart to share jokes in future.

Apart from being distracted and looking for fun at the wrong time, overall I think I was a good student. My English teacher was by far my favourite. Well-spoken, well-dressed, with thick, wavy, hair and an impressive handlebar moustache, which I am sure he proudly waxed every day, he was the one person who overlooked my failings and encouraged me to excel in the subject I loved best, English, writing essays and short stories.

Regrettably, my arithmetic teacher was the complete opposite. Tall, with big hands and hairy, gorilla-like arms, he had a bellowing voice and an intimidating long cane. He would pace up and down the aisles, his beady eyes surveying the class like an eagle homing in on its prey.

Suddenly, he would turn, thrash his victim's desk with the cane and bellow, "Eight times seven is …?" And if he received the correct answer, he would pounce on his next prey with another thwack of his cane and a different multiplication question or sum. And that, with increasing speed and ferocity, is how he conducted the lesson.

Despite his fearsome appearance and unorthodox ways, I suspect he was quite harmless because I never saw him use the cane to hit anyone. He only ever hit the desktops. But at the time, I was absolutely terrified of him and would spend the entire lesson trying to avoid his gaze, usually by lifting my desktop and hiding behind it, pretending to be looking for a book. Not surprisingly, I was very poor at arithmetic. Still am! That part of my brain was damaged for life. Anything related to sums or tables causes instant reverse brain activity, sometimes total brain-freeze.

One good thing about school was that we had free milk every day. One-third of a pint bottle with a silver top that we would press with our thumb to remove, or stab with a straw to make a hole to sip through. We also had free school meals, which were generally good, although I dreaded it when gorilla man was on duty.

He made us finish every morsel, even the greens, which tasted like stewed nothingness; and he would not allow us to leave the dining hall unless our plate was completely empty of food. So, we devised a clever trick to dodge him. If I had finished eating everything I liked, I would scrape the leftovers, usually the greens, onto the plate of the girl sitting next to me. I would then put my hand up and ask, "Sir, may I go please?" and show him my empty plate. And when he nodded that it was okay to go, I would politely say, "Thank you, Sir," and wait till he had passed on to another table. Hurriedly scraping my leftovers, and hers, back onto my plate, I would then race to the bin, dump the food, place the plate on the stack of used plates, and make a speedy exit.

One summer, during the holidays, Mum signed me up for school dinners. I loathed the idea of going all that way solely for a free meal. In my oversensitive, juvenile mind, it deepened the hurt and humiliation of being a struggling post-war family. Moreover, I was the only one having free dinners, or so I thought, because whenever I got there, it was only the dinner ladies and me.

Looking back though, I must admit I did dilly dally along the way, wishing with every hesitant step that the school would be closed when I got there, so inevitably I arrived when the others had already been and left.

So averse was I to having those free school meals, I would walk part of the way, turn around and go straight back home, but when Mum questioned me about the meal, what I had eaten, I had no answer, so she quickly guessed I had not been to school and sent me back again. Dragging my feet along the ground, I trod the dreaded path once more, wishing the pavement would swallow me up or that a sudden gust of wind would carry me away on a magic carpet to any place but school.

Sunday school was always a happy time and place for me. I loved listening to stories from the Bible, especially stories about Jesus and the parables he told his followers. I loved the gospel songs, too. Songs like, *Jesus loves me, this I know, for the Bible tells me so*; *What a friend we have in Jesus*; *Jesus is calling, calling for you and for me*; and many more.

Once, when a teacher was absent due to illness, I was asked to look after the tiny tots. After getting them to sing some of their favourite songs, I told them a story I had recently written about the consequences of telling lies and how ultimately the truth is revealed. They loved it, and their enthusiastic clapping at the end encouraged me to write similar moral-based stories.

Occasionally, our Sunday school arranged excursions, picnics in the countryside or by the sea. By far the most memorable for me was a trip to the zoo. Dressed in our Sunday best, we excitedly lined up beside the coach, which we called a charabanc. Most of us had never been on a charabanc before. I can still hear the joyous chanting, "We're all going to the zoo today and we're going in a charabanc!"

It was a glorious summer day, and we had all the time in the world to have our picnic lunch and enjoy every corner of the zoo. We wandered leisurely past the cages, gazing in wonder at animals we had never even heard of before. We were even more amazed to see wallabies grazing freely on the grassy slopes, darting behind bushes whenever we tried to get close. And on the same hilltop, we discovered a stone wishing chair.

As everyone took turns to make a wish, I remember wondering what to wish for. This I knew, it had to be something special and meaningful. I waited until everyone else had made their wish and then sat on the hard stone seat, eyes tightly closed, silently waiting for inspiration. And then it came! A wish from the deepest part of me! And in a whisper not even the birds could hear, I said, "I wish I may always be near to God."

Many happy childhood hours were spent in Sunday School. I also spent many pleasurable evenings in missionary meetings, which were held once a week in a church member's home. The main purpose of the meetings was to sew clothes, mostly frocks as I recall, for missionaries to take back with them to Africa, India or wherever they were stationed. We sewed by hand. Every stitch a prayer.

Once, a missionary on furlough from India came to tell us about her work. She showed us a brightly coloured sari. "Come!" she said, signalling to me. "Let me show you how women in India dress."

She draped the yards of fine cotton material around my waist, making several pleats in the front. She then put the end part over my head. Although the material was very fine, it felt warm. It felt mine, and I wished I could keep it.

Fledglings All

Like a fast train, primary and junior school days came and went, and with the start of grammar school, life in our neighbourhood changed profoundly. No more games around the shelter. No more adventures in our Wild West or treks along the Quaggy.

Once spending all our playtime together, we were now going our separate ways, to different schools in different places. And as if to validate the sad truth that our childhood days were over, we learnt that our old witch had died.

Life at home was different, too. When we were little, we would huddle together in the living room, in front of the coal fire in winter or on the large sofa on warm summer days when the hearth was bare; and we would share food and stories without any inhibitions. And sharing a bed with siblings, the smell and warmth of our bodies mingling, was an indescribable and priceless experience.

But now, we all went to different schools or workplaces and life was all comings and goings. We had meals together, but then went off in different directions to do our own important things. Mine was mostly homework, which I had nearly every day.

I now shared a bed with my oldest sister, the one who scared us in Greenwich tunnel. And I shared her clothes, too, although she didn't know it. Not for some time, at least. But one day, I was happily skipping along the road, wearing one of her very stylish blouses and matching full-flared skirt, feeling bold and beautiful, and as I turned the corner into the high street, I bumped right into her.

Moments of embarrassing silence as she recognised the outfit but didn't know what to say. Several years older than me, she was the mainstay of our family. A second mother, you might say. I admired and looked up to her; and like my younger sister, she was kind and caring. When I got home, she simply told me to ask next time I wanted to wear any of her clothes. But after that, I never dared.

<hr>

No longer children, we were all fledglings preparing to leave the nest, some sooner, others later. Sad, but that's the way things were in our small world, just as it is in the world at large.

At grammar school, if I was a serious student, I was also a fantasist. In class, my mind would often drift, silently transporting me faraway. Walking to and from school, my mind was all too often lost in the clouds; and not looking where I was going, I would bump into someone or something, usually a lamp post.

For the first time, I had to wear a uniform, which I rather liked, except for the velour hat that kept slipping off my head or blowing away on blustery days, although it did help to soften the blow on those all too frequent lamp post encounters.

I became very keen on sports, so much so that everyone thought I would end up being a Physical Education teacher. True, I could swim, play tennis and badminton, and was in the school hockey and netball teams, but I had no plans of making a career in sports. At that time, I had no career plans at all. I simply wanted to enjoy school and do as well as I could.

My best friend in secondary school was a Jamaican girl, the only coloured girl in our year, probably in the entire school. She had bright expressive eyes, usually full of mischief, but occasionally sad and soulful. Her generous lips seemed to be forever smiling, and her frizzy hair fascinated me. With her wild sense of humour and infectious laughter, she reminded me of my partner in crime of earlier schooldays. We were a match made in heaven!

Linking arms and putting left foot forward, we would often skip along the corridor, giggling and singing, "I left, I left. I had a good wife and I left." But once, a teacher caught us in the act and gave us a "black mark" for rowdiness and for running in the corridor where walking only was allowed. A black mark was awarded for serious misdemeanours and appeared on the annual report, so that quickly put an end to our corridor shenanigans.

There were times when my Jamaican friend's mood was unusually sombre, and she would confide in me the problems she and her family faced. Some neighbours treated them with contempt, and said insulting, hurtful things.

Having grown up with the belief that we are all children of God and that we should love our neighbours, I found it not only difficult to comprehend but extremely upsetting. My friend was good-hearted, generous, lively, and full of fun. Highly intelligent and talented, too, with so much to give, to strive for and achieve. Why couldn't everyone see that?

She once asked me, "Why did God make me black? Why not white, like you?"

At first, I was lost for words. I had never questioned why I was white, but then I had never experienced racism, whereas she had. It took me a while to answer.

"Well, God doesn't only make black and white," I said cheerfully. "Look at the butterflies and birds! The world is full of colourful things, and black is just as beautiful as white. Take horses, for example. What colour of horse is most admired?"

"I don't know," she said. "You tell me."

"Black!" I emphatically replied. "Horses can be many different colours, but ask anyone which colour they like best, and I bet you most will say black. Remember the story of Black Beauty? Didn't everyone love him?"

Barely had I spoken those words when a sudden twinge of guilt brought back memories of our poor old witch. How we tormented her because she wore black. I turned again to my friend.

"And do you know what else I think?"

Her dark, expressive eyes met mine, perhaps wondering what tangent my thoughts would take next.

"Well, I think superstition is to blame. Why are people scared of witches? Because they are always dressed in black. They also have black cauldrons, black crows, and black cats. You see, darkness is black, isn't it? Everyone is afraid of the dark, so that's probably why people are afraid of anything black.

"People also fear the unknown or anything that is different. Where you come from, everyone is black. You are all the same. But here, people are mostly white, so you look different.

"God made some people black, some white and others in between. And He made them different for a reason. Maybe it is all to do with the sun. Less sunshine makes people's skin white; more sunshine makes it darker. People lie in the sun to get a tan, don't they? So, it could be as simple as that.

"And what about Adam and Eve?" I asked.

"What do you mean?" she responded, wondering where this was leading. "What about Adam and Eve?"

"Well, were they black or white? God never told us in the Bible. For all we know, they could have been black. But black or white, what difference does it make? God made people of different colours, so all are beautiful."

⋯⟡⋯

I was just a schoolgirl then. What did I know about the world and racial discrimination? One thing I was sure of, though. There was no justification for it, and it was very wrong.

Many years later, several cases of police brutality against black people hit the world headlines, highlighting the appalling extent of race and colour discrimination in today's world. Over the years, I had given much thought to this universal conundrum. Was it in any way analogous to pack mentality? Scaring off or attacking those that don't belong, look different or don't conform.

Animals that live in social groups are protective of their family and will fiercely defend it against intruders. They establish a pecking order that determines which animal has the strength, stamina, and physique to be the dominant leader, a strategy that works very well for them. The stronger the family group, the better they can defend their home and territory.

But we are human beings, not animals, and as such have been elevated to the highest position on this earth. We are its custodians. So how have our hearts and minds been sabotaged? What has robbed us of tolerance, kindness, sympathy, and empathy? What makes us behave more like animals and less like human beings?

The juxtaposition of these tragic and brutal assaults on innocent black people, alongside very fond memories of my beautiful Jamaican schoolfriend, inspired me to write the following poem.

Colour-blind

My neighbour is black, and I am white.
Some say we are as different as day and night.
But I am colour-blind and cannot see
Any difference between my neighbour
and me.

***

Character does not depend on colour of skin.
Colour does not define us, nor cause us to sin.
The sinful have evil and darkness within,
The pure have goodness and light within,
Regardless of race and kith and kin.

***

We all have the right to achieve and succeed.
We share similar dreams, have similar needs.
We all have the same colour blood flowing
through.
We breathe the same air, share the same
world, too,

***

My neighbour is black, and I am white.
But are we truly as different as day and night?
Because I am colour-blind, I cannot see
Any difference between my neighbour
and me.

⊰───◈───⊱

Back to schooldays!

Now, whoever prepared the timetable for the GCE O level exams did not consider the weather and its effect on the young candidates. Exams should be in winter when people are already indoors because of the cold. But no! The exams are during summer when young and old alike crave the warmth and freedom of the sunny outdoors. Students are supposed to ignore all the exciting activities around them and bury their heads in their books instead.

Revision was a real struggle for me. Although I had prepared a revision timetable, keeping to it was far from easy. I would spend more time daydreaming than revising. However, incredible as it may seem, help was literally around the corner.

There was a church on the way to school with a huge notice board outside. Normally, it displayed a quotation from the Bible, but this time it read: *It is not the number of hours you put into the work that counts but the amount of work you put into the hours.*

Those words could not have come at a better time. It was as though God had put them there especially for me. From then onwards, if I revised for one hour only, it was an hour of concentrated work with no daydreaming. And it paid off. I passed in all subjects, except Maths, for which I mostly blame my primary school teacher.

Sixth form and A-level studies! I had chosen English Literature, Domestic Science and Geography. Sixth form was as exciting as Eton Mess or Chelsea buns – for the privileged elite. That is how I felt. We had our own common room, complete with table and armchairs and an electric kettle for making our own tea or coffee.

We were still provided with free milk every day but had to share in the cost of a packet of tea or jar of instant coffee. Since we could not afford to buy sugar as well, we all developed a taste for coffee or tea without. And in my case, it became a lifelong habit.

After considering several career possibilities, and frankly there was not much choice for girls in those days, I decided to become a teacher and secured a provisional place in teacher training college. Although my academic success was trivial in the scale of great achievements, the effect on me was as euphoric as if I had climbed Mount Everest.

The last day of school is one of those milestones no one ever forgets. The farewells and good wishes, the sense of accomplishment and aspirations for the future. And when the huge oak doors, darkened by years by rain and city dust, closed behind me for the last time, I remember feeling exhilarated, and for no apparent reason a song rose to my mind which I sang to myself all the way home.

"I know where I'm going. I know who's going with me. I know who I am, and the man I'm going to marry."

That song, like a record on automatic replay, echoed in my mind for days on end. Romance and marriage were far from my mind, but I *did* know where I was going. I was off to teacher training college. Ironically, however, the words of that song were totally untrue for me, as unfolding events were about to demonstrate.

Serendipity

Just a few weeks remained to pack and say my goodbyes to family and friends. Sunday came and I went to church where I sang in the alto section of the choir. I was also a member of the youth club, held after the Sunday evening service. There would be dancing, badminton and table tennis, and occasionally our minister would invite a guest to give a lecture on some topic of general interest.

As I entered the church vestibule, I noticed two dark strangers. Asian, I thought, and probably followers of the Hindu religion. But that prompted the question, why were they attending a Christian church service? I took my place in the choir, opened my hymn book, and thought no more about them.

After the service, the youth members' transformation from worshipper to reveller was spontaneous. I generally preferred to sit and watch the others. In school, I loved country and Scottish dancing, but here it was Rock and Roll, and I had neither the craze nor the panache that everyone else possessed.

Amidst all the merriment, our minister arrived and clapped his hands in the air to get everyone's attention. And that is when I saw them again. The two dark strangers.

"I would like to introduce you to two new members of our church, Mohammad and Mustafa, so please welcome them. Mohammad has agreed to talk to you about his home country, Pakistan, so please be seated everyone."

The minister then took his leave, and Mohammad's eyes followed him until he was sure he was gone and out of earshot.

"First, I would like to explain," he said in a hushed voice, "that we are not new members of the church. We happen to live down the road and we came to ask the minister if we could play badminton and table tennis. He said we could, but only if we attended the church service. So, here we are!"

And like a mischievous schoolboy who had played a prank on a teacher and got away with it, he smiled. And of course, we all laughed and promised not to tell.

Mohammad talked less about Pakistan, which none of us had ever heard of before, and more about his religion. He was not a Hindu as I had first imagined but a Muslim. Smiling every time he paused, he explained very lucidly the principles of a Muslim's life, known as the Five Pillars of Islam.

1. Declaration of Faith (belief in One God),
2. Obligatory Prayers,

3. Compulsory Giving (alms),
4. Fasting,
5. and Pilgrimage.

He also explained how to do *wudhu*, the special ablution performed before saying prayers or reading the Muslim's Holy Book, the Quran.

While the others seemed more eager to get back to the dancing and other activities, I was listening attentively. Mohammad must have noticed because afterwards he came and sat down on the vacant chair beside me.

"You seemed very interested," he said. "Would you like to know more about Islam? I have some books I can give you if you like."

I replied that I would, so he gave me his address and invited me to come any time. I thanked him and then he and his friend Mustafa, who didn't utter a word all evening, went off to play table tennis, leaving me with much to mull over.

A devout Christian, I belonged to a Bible group known as Scripture Union and proudly wore its little metal badge, green and gold with an Aladdin-like lamp engraved on it. However, I had recently begun to question many things about my religion. How can Jesus be the son of God? Why would God want a son? Or a daughter, for that matter?

People become old and die, plants and animals do too, so there is a perpetual need for flora, fauna, and human beings to procreate, to preserve the habitat and population on earth. That is the circle of our lives. God alone is the Creator of all things. He is eternal, so what need has He of progeny?

But perhaps most confusing for me was the concept of the trinity, the Father, the Son, and the Holy Ghost, or Spirit. How can one be three and three be one? And how can they be one and the same? Also, the notion that mere belief in any being could guarantee redemption and wash away my sins, didn't appeal to me.

I had been brought up to understand consequences, accountability, punishment and reward, dependant on one's conduct. It made no sense to me that whatever sins a man may commit, he is forgiven if he professes belief in a particular prophet or saint. Also, when we can talk directly to God, any time, any place, then what need is there of a mediator? So, at an age when the insouciance of youth normally abounds, I found myself lost in deeply spiritual contemplation.

⁕⸺⬥⬥⸺⁕

It did not take me long to decide that I *would* pay Mohammad and Mustafa a visit and listen to what they had to say about religion. Perhaps they could answer some of my questions and set my mind at ease. It didn't occur to me then that being of a different country, culture, and religion, they were probably the last people to ask.

So, the following afternoon, I stood on the doorstep of Mohammad's house and knocked, but there was no answer.

I stepped back and waited. Still, no one came. All the curtains were drawn, so perhaps they were sleeping late, or not at home. I was about to leave when I noticed there was another door, down several steps to the basement.

Nervously clutching my duffel bag, second thoughts about the wisdom of being there creeping into my head, I wondered if I should knock or leave, but then the door opened, and Muhammed popped his head out. He invited me in, his eyes impishly bright and his winsome smile revealing the wide gap between his two front teeth.

The front door led straight into the living room, which was dark and had a strong, unfamiliar smell. I felt a little uneasy, feelings Mohammad must have noticed because whilst I was taking my shoes off, he drew back the curtains, allowing the light of day to rush in. Very politely, he then offered me a chair.

Feeling somewhat more at ease, I looked around. Mustafa was sitting quietly on the sofa. I thought he looked sad, or perhaps he was not pleased to see me, although he did say hello and asked me how I was. The room itself surprised me. It was not cluttered or untidy but neat and tastefully furnished. Not at all what I expected of two young bachelors. I assumed they were bachelors.

The first thing I noticed when removing my shoes at the doorway was the flooring. From wall to wall, it was covered with a luxurious off-white carpet with random streaks of different colours, a design I had never seen before nor since. An elegant sofa was the showpiece of the room. It was of modern design with loose, dark brown cushions with flecks of colour that blended well with the carpet, and a wooden frame with extending flaps both ends that served as side-tables, big enough for a cup and saucer and bowl of snacks. A matching coffee table stood on a small rug in the middle of the room.

On one side, against the wall, was a divan with two red velvet bolster cushions with golden tassels, and alongside the opposite wall was a low bookcase with a variety of books, some written in English, others with strange, golden writing on the thick spine, which I guessed were books about Islam. And on the top shelf of the bookcase was a tiny, glazed pot with burning joss sticks, thin twirls of smoke drifting towards the ceiling, leisurely embracing everything in the room, the source of the fragrance that had greeted me.

The living room, I later discovered, led into a small hallway, with the kitchen and then a bathroom on the right, and a flight of stairs to the first level and two generous bedrooms. Another flight of stairs led to two further bedrooms, both let out to lodgers.

While Mustafa remained sitting, Mohammad moved in and out of the kitchen preparing tea, which he served with a dish of *halva*. Garnished with almonds and pistachios, it looked and tasted delicious and like nothing I had ever had before. It was a traditional dessert in India and Pakistan, he explained, made from butter, sugar, and semolina.

"I can show you how to make it," he offered. "It's very easy and quick to make."

Mohammad, it turned out, was an excellent cook. He knew how to make curry dishes and chapatis, and when I told him I had no idea what chapatis were, he promised to make some next time I came, and a curry as well, of course.

I was completely overawed. I felt I had been transported to another world. To the land of the Arabian Nights or somewhere equally thrilling! Mustafa offered me more halva, and Mohammad placed two books on the table, which helped bring me back down to earth. One book was entitled, *The Five Pillars of Islam*. The other was an English translation of the Holy Quran.

"These are for you," he said. "You don't have to return them. You can keep them. They're yours."

I was about to thank him, but he spoke first, reminding me that I had expressed interest in knowing more about Islam, and asking if I would like him to tell me, here and now?

"Well, I'm not in any hurry. I suppose I have time right now," I answered. So he began.

"Let's start with prayer," he said. "All Muslims must pray five times a day. Before sunrise, at midday, late afternoon, immediately after sunset, and late evening before going to bed."

Mohammad must have heard my gasp because he paused. I went to church every Sunday and said my prayers every day, but not five times. "Do you really pray five times a day?" I asked. "Where do you pray? I mean, do you have a place of worship, like we have a church?"

"Prayers are compulsory," he replied. "Missing prayers is a sin, so we try our best to say all five prayers. In Pakistan it was easy. We would hear the *adhan*, the call to prayer, and then go to the nearest mosque. But here, our mosque is quite far away and calling the adhan out loud is not allowed, so we usually pray at home."

He placed the books in my hands. "Read them, if you're interested and can find the time."

"Oh, yes. I'll definitely read them," I assured him, taking this as a cue to end my visit, which had lasted much longer than I had intended. I had planned to stop by, pick up the books he had mentioned during our first meeting in the church, and then leave. But here I was, almost two hours later, my mind awhirl, and my own burning questions unspoken. Next time, I promised myself, as I finally took my leave.

Winds of Change

In those timeless days, freedom flowed like a gentle, meandering stream from childhood through to adolescence. Time in post-war Britain, when churchgoer or not people generally had the fear of God in their hearts, and youngsters feared even more their parent's wrath! There were family rules and a common trust that those rules would not be broken.

In our family, the rules were simple. Tell when and where you are going, don't get into any trouble, and be back by teatime. Mum would often add, "and don't do anything I wouldn't do", which was wide open to interpretation. But we were lucky. There was little to distract us then. Not like today's challenging world where there are drinks, drugs, social media, and all manner of activities to tempt us.

My mother was somewhat concerned when I told her my plan to go to Mohammad's house again. "Why do you want to get involved with foreigners," she asked.

I honestly didn't know what to reply. And I didn't think she or anyone else would understand the pressing need I had to find answers, to clear away the doubts about my faith. Youth has its failings, lack of patience being one of them, impetuosity another.

So, there I was, once more knocking on the basement door. To my surprise, this time Mustafa opened it and a new aroma wafted towards me, piquant like the joss sticks but very different. It was, I soon learnt, the smell of Indian spices. True to his word, Mohammad, still busy in the kitchen, was cooking mushroom curry and waiting to show me how to make chapatis.

I watched, fascinated, as he rolled the dough into little balls, and then flattened and patted them with his hands until they were about the size of a dinner plate. It was even more amazing the way he expertly flipped it onto the very hot iron griddle, or *tawa* as he called it, turned it over several times and then pressed it with a cloth, gently coaxing it to puff up like a football.

When everything was laid out on the coffee table, we sat cross-legged on the soft rug around it and prepared to eat. *"Bismillah!"* said Mohammad and Mustafa.

"Bismillah means, *we begin with the Name of Allah,"* Mohammad explained. "We say this before we commence anything, like eating, prayers, and work."

"Bismillah!" I repeated, wanting to be polite and to please. But how to proceed? There were no spoons, no knives, or forks. Mohammad, forever alert, noticed my quandary.

"We eat like this," he said, taking a piece of chapati, wrapping it around a small piece of mushroom and popping it into his mouth. "But right hand only. We always eat food with our right hand, never the left."

Simple for him, I thought, but not so for me, and while we were eating, I could not help noticing their fingers were not messy like mine. I was determined, however, to master this new way of eating.

"How is the curry?" Mohammad asked. "I hope it's not too spicy for you." And from across the table Mustafa glanced at me, waiting for me to answer.

"It's delicious," I replied, "Very spicy, but nice." And I discovered a way to offset the spiciness – a large piece of chapati with only a tiny portion of curry.

They started to clear the table, and I was about to get up when Mohammad politely told me to stay sitting. "There's more," he said, and I wondered what they were going to offer me next. Being treated like an honoured guest was something so novel to me and completely overwhelming.

Hastily, as though they feared I might run away, they reset the table with three small dessert dishes and a bowl of what appeared to be peaches, cut into small chunks, swimming in thick juice or syrup, and a small jug of fresh cream. And this time there were spoons.

"Please, have some," said Mohammed, handing me a dish. "It's our favourite fruit, mango. This is from a tin, but at home in summer we would have fresh ones nearly every day. An Englishman once said, 'If you want to eat mangoes you need to sit in the bathtub'. That's because they are so soft and the juice oozes out all over you. But this is much easier to eat and tastes almost as good."

What to say! My taste buds were really being challenged and entertained. The delight of the sweet mango with fresh cream was such a contrast to the hot spiciness of the curry. Nothing but a mango tastes like a mango. The closest comparison might be that it is a cross between a peach and a pineapple, or between a peach and a pear.

"Did you manage to read the book about Islam," Mohammad asked over the cup of tea that followed.

"Yes, I did, and I found it very interesting," was my honest reply.

Now it was my turn to ask a question. "Mohammad, can I ask you something. It's not about the book. It's about Christianity."

"Yes, of course. We both attended missionary school, so we know about the Bible and Christian beliefs." He then paused so I could speak.

I hesitated, fearful of sounding blasphemous. And then I asked, "Do you believe Jesus is the son of God?"

Mohammad's reply was prompt and decisive. "Absolutely not! The Holy Quran is an integral part of our faith, and it contains a chapter that we also recite in our daily prayers. It says, *'God is One. He begot no one and Himself is not begotten'.*

Look it up in the English version of the Quran I gave you, chapter 112. And in many other verses of the Quran, God condemns those who claim He has a son."

"That's what I thought," I replied, thankful to be freed of the doubts that had been preying on my mind. "But what about the trinity, the Father, the Son, and the Holy Spirit?"

Again, Mohammad answered without hesitation. "There is no trinity. How can there be? God is One. So, being One, there is no son, nor holy spirit. People distort religion, to mislead others or to suit their own purpose. In Prophet Mohammad's time, some even claimed the angels were God's daughters.

"In many religions, people believe there is only one God but claim their self-made idols or gods are mediators. They also believe that to please God, they must first please their idols by offering prayers, food, and animal sacrifices. But we do not need a mediator. We enjoy the privilege of praying and speaking directly to God.

"The Kaaba, or House of God, in Mecca was full of useless idols, and during pre-Islamic times, all manner of obscenities were practised in the name of religion. Can you imagine, people would even walk around the Kaaba completely naked as a form of worship? So, you see, people have always made-up nonsensical things about religion, just to fool others or for their own satisfaction.

"Jesus called God, 'Father'. But when Christians recite The Lord's Prayer, they say, 'Our Father Who art in heaven'. In a sense, God is everyone's Father. After all, He created Adam, and we all descend from Adam. And remember this, Jesus did not speak English. He spoke Aramaic. And in Aramaic, the word for God can also be translated into 'father'.

"Like you, I believe in Jesus, not as the son of God but the son of Mary. We call her Maryam, by the way. And I believe in Jesus as a prophet. Jesus was given the Gospels. Mohammad was given the Holy Quran, which is the Holy Book all Muslims follow.

"Now, tell me one thing. If you are studying science from a book, given the choice, would you read an old edition of the book or the latest edition?"

"The latest edition, of course," I promptly replied.

"Why?" he asked.

I was beginning to understand Mohammad. He was impish but astute. Perhaps he was trying to trick me, so I took a little time to think before answering. "Because the latest edition would have been edited and updated, and any errors will have been eliminated."

"Exactly!" he said, clearly delighted. "As a Christian, you follow the Bible, which is the old edition of God's Book. It is old because God sent it to Jesus who preceded Prophet Muhammad. Also, much of the original Gospel has been altered or lost.

"I follow the latest edition of God's Book, the Holy Quran. And not only is it the latest edition, but it is also the last and final message. God has promised to protect it from any corruption or change. He also tells us that He will not send any more prophets.

"In the Quran God says, 'You will find no change in my Message'. From Prophet Adam to Prophet Muhammad, the Divine Message has always been the same. It is man who has changed it.

"Another thing the Quran tells us about Jesus is that he did not die on the cross. God took him up to heaven, body, and soul. So, he is alive, awaiting the day when God will send him back to earth to complete his earthly life. He will come at a time when the world is in total chaos, when religion has been forgotten. And he will lead the people with fairness and justice according to God's Laws, the laws of Islam."

I sat quietly for some time, overwhelmed by feelings impossible to describe. "You might not believe this, but before I met you, I prayed, asking God to show me the truth. I then had a dream in which I saw Jesus, and he told me, 'Don't worry! I will show you the way.'

"I know it was just a dream, but I believe God is showing me the way, through you two. Otherwise, how do you explain our chance meeting at the church? You only wanted to play badminton and table tennis, but I wanted answers about my Christian beliefs."

My words were met with silence; and unbeknown to me then, the seeds of Islam had been firmly planted.

A Bizarre Proposal

The next chapter of my life was not what I had imagined. So much had happened since leaving school, when the song, "I know where I'm going," kept resonating in my mind. Now, I was not sure where I was going, and I could not shake off feelings of uncertainty.

College was good. I attended lectures and tutorials and did all my assignments. It was a mixed college, and I remember feeling self-conscious when a male student commented on my pastry-white legs. During his youth club talk, Mohammad had told us it is forbidden for Muslim women to expose their bodies, and here was I, doing gymnastics wearing next to nothing and playing netball in a sleeveless tunic that was way above my knees.

Mohammad wrote to me occasionally, and when I went to collect my mail one day, the other students stood aside and made way for me. At first, I wondered if perhaps I had done something amiss. There was only one letter for me, and in place of "Miss" before my name, the word "Princess" was written in handwriting I did not recognise. I was speechless. Was that the reason everyone had made way for me?

The letter was from Mustafa. The quiet, shy one, who served me and observed me when I visited their home, but barely spoke. In the letter, he wrote that he hoped I was enjoying college life and looked forward to seeing me again during the half-term break.

There was a surprise awaiting me at Mohammad's. I say Mohammad's because although the house belonged to both, it was Mohammad who did most of the teaching and talking, as well as the cooking. Mustafa occasionally talked about his studies or his prize possession, a home projector, but generally he remained quiet.

After a cup of tea with halwa, in which he had mixed diced mango, combining my two favourite desserts, Mohammad presented me with gifts, recently arrived from Pakistan via a friend. I was speechless. An emerald, green sari, and a beige prayer mat with beautiful embroidery and a fringe of golden threads. Unaccustomed to receiving gifts, my first impulse was to politely refuse them, but neither of them would hear of it.

"No, they are for you," Mohammad insisted. "You *have* to take them," prudently omitting the fact that these very special gifts had not been easy to acquire. And had I known then that they were obtained under false pretext for Mustafa's *teacher,* I might not have accepted them.

"Let me show you how to wear it," said Mohammad, and he began to unravel yard after yard of the delicate sari.

Watching him triggered memories of the time a missionary dressed me in an Indian sari, except that this was not cotton but fine, shot silk, shimmering from green to purple as the light rays impishly danced over it. A richly embroidered border ran all along the hem, and the rest was plain, except for the end, about a yard of which was decorated to match the beautiful border.

I had never seen anything so exquisite. And to think that it was mine! In his letter to me, Mustafa addressed me as princess, and now here was Mohammad presenting me with a beautiful sari fit for a queen.

I watched attentively as Mohammad gathered the sari around his waist, knotted two ends together and began tucking it inside his trouser waistband. Twirling around, he draped it completely around him. In the front, he made several pleats, tucked them into his waist and threw the decorative end, which he called the *pallu*, over his shoulder. And then, like a model on a catwalk, pretending to be wearing high-heeled shoes by walking on tip toes, he strutted around the room trailing the pallu behind him while Mustafa and I watched and applauded.

He took the sari off and carefully folded it. "Now, shall I show you how we pray?" And he unrolled the prayer mat and placed it on the floor.

"The first rule is to make sure we place the mat facing *Qibla*, which is the direction towards Kaaba, the House of God in Mecca."

Adjusting the mat to the correct position, Mohammad then stood on it, his bare feet slightly apart. He began by holding both hands close to his ears, and then clasped his hands, right over left, in front of his waist. Next, head bowed and hands on knees; and then back up to a standing position. Down again, this time onto his knees, his forehead touching the mat. This he did twice, and then back to the kneeling position to recite the rest of the prayer. And all the time, he gave a running commentary, explaining each position.

This was a way of praying I had never witnessed before. Despite being complex, I thought it was disciplined and purposeful. Soon after, I said my thanks and goodbyes and left, taking the prayer mat with me, but not the sari. When was I ever going to wear it? Where would I wear it? And I also wondered, and perhaps feared, what my mother would say.

Back at college the letters from Mustafa, still addressed to 'Princess', continued to arrive. He had asked for my help with a course subject he found very dull, Production Engineering. He said it was neither scientific nor mathematical and that he could not understand why he had to study it. So, I answered questions or rephrased them to make it easier for him to memorise. He had also asked me to teach him French, although I later came to know that not a single exercise I had set for him had been done.

If I had not met Mustafa and Mohammad when I did, I probably would have settled down to college life. But I didn't. I felt a misfit, and each visit to their home seemed to draw me further away from the career path I had chosen, and I began to wonder why.

I was a practicing Christian, so why was it so easy to accept and follow whatever I learnt about their religion? There was no compulsion. They were never assertive. Not once, did either of them compel me to do this or follow that. So why? And then the answer came to me. Whatever I had felt was lacking in Christianity, I found in Islam. More than that, I embraced and welcomed it. I had arrived at the crossroads and could no longer claim, 'I know where I'm going'.

Every night, I would sit cross-legged on the prayer mat, read the Bible, and then pray. One night, I prayed well into the night, a candle flickering on the floor in front of me. It was one of those rare moments when, deeply absorbed in prayer, you feel sublime peace. The next day, I wrote this poem.

Paradise

If there be Paradise on earth, then surely
it is here,
Where, kneeling on a simple mat, I say my
prayers.
When the spirit dwelling deep within awakens
And embraces every part, and wraps my heart
In the sweet fragrance of holy bliss.
If there be Paradise on earth, then surely
it is this.

***

With countless pleasures life is blessed.
The singing of a babbling brook, thrilling
tales within a book.
Lovers walking hand in hand, cool waters
rippling on the sand.
Clouds and rainbows in the sky, exotic
birds, and butterflies.
Fields of never-ending green, maidens pure
of lovesome mien.
Flowers abiding in the sun; pleasures surely
everyone.

***

But here! Bowed in silent adoration,
Bereft of body, self and will,
Bathed in the sweet aura of Thy Presence,
calm and still.
If there be Paradise on earth, then surely
it is this.

Every visit to Mohammad's brought new surprises for me,
but nothing could have prepared me for the next one. It was
raining steadily and as I entered I noticed Mustafa was not
in his usual place on the sofa. "Where's Mustafa," I asked,
more out of politeness than interest.

"Outside," Mohammad replied.

"Outside?" I repeated. "Did he have to go somewhere?"

"No! Here outside! He's in the garden," was his surprising reply.

Of course, I did not believe him. Who would be outside in the rain, and why, unless they had a shed or conservatory? But then he led me through the kitchen to a door that opened onto the garden. And there, sitting on an old, discarded sofa was Mustafa, not surprisingly looking rain-drenched, and so lost in thought I don't think he noticed me.

"What's he doing," I whispered, trying to imagine why anyone would choose to sit in the rain. His answer hit me like a bombshell!

"He wants to marry you," was his reply, "He's too shy to ask you himself, so he's asked me to tell you. He says he'll only come back inside if you agree."

To say I was dumbstruck is a massive understatement. What a strange way to propose! These two had obviously been influenced by the most romantic era in Indian film history, where heroes serenaded their beloved, wooing her secretly and openly, preferring death to life without her.

Marriage to either of them though, or to anyone for that matter, was far from my mind. I half suspected it might be a joke, but just to be sure and to coax him out of the rain, I said, "Please call him inside and we can talk about it."

Mustafa was dead serious though, which sent my mind awhirl once more, searching for a solution to this unforeseen dilemma. It was post-war London, the exciting sixties when anything and everything was possible. But marriage to a man from a country the other side of the world! Different upbringing and culture! I needed time to assimilate and process it all, far more time than Mustafa seemed willing to give. Marriage was obviously on his mind, but it definitely wasn't on mine.

Knowing I had to do something there and then, I suddenly had a zany idea. If Mustafa agreed, we would exchange watches. I would wear his for a few days, and he would wear mine. Maybe, I thought, just the feel of it would help me to decide if I should accept his proposal or decline? Mustafa agreed. So, he wore my delicate, gold-plated bracelet watch, and I wore his rather chunky Favre-Leuba.

<hr>

At the crossroads once more. Except that it was more like a maze, twisting and turning, the way out forever eluding me. We returned the watches, and I could not help smiling, amused at the thought of his willingness to wear my fancy watch, and at my crazy idea in the first instance to base my answer to his proposal on the mere feel of a watch. But he had worn it in earnest, in the hope of a positive outcome. He wanted an answer, and I could see in his eyes how much it meant to him.

I had worn his watch, hidden beneath my sleeve, for one week. Despite being rather heavy, it had felt warm and comfortable. It belonged to someone good and sincere, I thought, but that was not enough to commit myself to marriage. So, I asked for one more day to pray for the right answer.

I lit a candle and sat on my prayer mat. I still had not learnt to pray the Muslim way, but I had replaced the Bible with the English translation of the Holy Quran. I read a few pages, prayed for guidance, and then went to sleep, hoping for inspiration, a revealing dream, something, anything, that would help me to decide.

I awoke none the wiser. But two thoughts were foremost in my mind. Firstly, while I could find no reason to say yes, I could find no reason to say no either. Secondly, I had fully embraced my new-found faith. I wanted to learn more about Islam and follow its teachings, but I needed someone to guide me.

Was this a golden opportunity? A gift from God! If I refused Mustafa, what were my chances of meeting another Muslim who would ask me to marry him? Very unlikely, I thought. I was not the gregarious type. In social circles, I was reserved and kept myself to myself.

I remember, when I was in sixth form, there was a girl I thought rather mannish and unattractive. She even had hair on her chest and was undergoing hormonal treatment. Yet she had a handsome, blond-haired boyfriend, and I could not figure out how or why. What did her boyfriend see in her? What did they have in common? What was the chemistry between them? It completely baffled me.

And then came the inevitable question. Why didn't I have a boyfriend? which I answered myself. I was not looking for one. It seemed equally clear to me that boys were not attracted to me. And that is when I labelled myself plain, mousy, and unattractive.

Mustafa must have seen something in me, though. He had shown his desire to marry me in such a bizarre manner. With my future career occupying my mind, marriage had certainly not been a part of my plan. Undeniably, it was a serious proposal, and a few weeks later, I took a gargantuan leap of faith and agreed.

But all was not free sailing. Disaster struck several weeks later in the form of a letter from Mustafa's Bai Jan, in Urdu of course, but the gist is what follows.

What was he thinking? he had asked. Everyone's shocked. Mother cries every time anyone mentions your name. She has been waiting and praying for your return and had two cousins lined up for you to choose from, and then you send word that you are planning to marry a British girl. That's not why father sent you to England. Besides, English girls are very different. They are not subservient like our girls. And if you do marry this girl, we fear you may never come back home to Pakistan.

So, the marriage must be off, I thought. But not so! Mustafa wrote back almost immediately, assuring them that the girl he had chosen was not like the girls they had heard about. She had even become a Muslim, and he had no reason to doubt her character or her loyalty. As for his cousins, he was not interested in marrying either of them, never had been. The letter was stamped and posted, and we all waited, not knowing what news the next letter would bring.

Meanwhile, Mustafa presented me with a gift, through Mohammad because he was still too shy to give it to me himself. It was a small golden packet containing a very fine, cotton handkerchief with embroidered flowers in one corner.

"Thank you," I said. "It's very pretty."

Mohammad (and Mustafa, of course) was eager for me to take it out of the packet. "Open it!" he said.

I soon realised this was not a handkerchief meant for ordinary use, but a keepsake and token of his affection. Scrawled across one corner of the handkerchief Mustafa had written, *my faith in you.*

Still on tenterhooks, waiting for that all important letter from Bhai Jan, Mohammad kept reassuring us that all would be fine. He decided it might be a good time to choose a Muslim name for me. His pet name for me was *Nuqta*, which simply means the punctuation mark, full stop. He used to tease me about my small button nose, and said that when God had finished making me, He put a full stop in the middle of my face.

"What do you think of the name, Layla," he asked. "Like in the legendary story of Layla and Majnu."

He then related a tragic story of two young lovers, an Arabian version of Romeo and Juliet. Qays and Layla were childhood sweethearts and when they grew up their love for one another deepened and Qays openly proclaimed his love in countless poems about her. So passionate were his efforts to woo her, he was given the nickname *Majnu*, meaning mad. Perhaps the origin of the saying, madly in love!

When Qays asked for Layla's hand in marriage, her father refused, saying it would be an utter disgrace for his daughter to marry a mad man. So, he married her off to a rich merchant. The heartbroken Majnu left his home and spent the rest of his life wandering in the desert. Not long after her marriage, Layla died of a broken heart. Majnu's dead body was later found lying next to her grave.

"What do you think?" asked Mohammad. "Would you like to change your name to Layla?"

I was not sure. I could see the parallels between Mustafa and Majnu, but the unhappy connotations of Layla's heartache and early death did little to recommend it. I was about say no when Mustafa turned to me and said, "I like the name, Layla. It suits you."

So, from that moment on, I was Layla.

⋅•⋅⋙✦⋘⋅•⋅

The long-awaited letter arrived, and it was good news. They had talked everything over and agreed that Mustafa had the right to marry whomever he chose, so he could go ahead.

77

Knowing how determined Mustafa was, I think they saw the wisdom of taking the path of least resistance because any argument on their part was destined to fail.

Although my parents were aware of my friendship with the foreign friends as they called them, I think they considered it a phase and a fad that would wear off sooner or later, so they were quite shocked when I told them I had agreed to marry Mustafa.

Ever the pragmatist, my father seemed far more disappointed that I was giving up my studies and less concerned that I was about to leave home and possibly fly halfway across the world. He had had high hopes for me, that I would obtain a degree or other professional qualification. My mother, however, was more concerned about the practical implications.

"But he is Pakistani, and there is such a cultural divide. If you had chosen a Frenchman, I would have understood. Frenchmen are still more like us. At least they are white and European. But a black man! That's a totally different matter," was her candid reply.

Mustafa was not black. In fact, with his dark brown hair and eyes, and lightly tanned complexion, many people mistook him for an Italian. But those were times when Enoch Powell was ranting and raving about the influx of immigrants, backed by most British voters, my own father included. So, whether they were from Africa or Asia, all immigrants were tainted with the same brush and labelled black.

Nevertheless, I had my mother's blessing. "I think you will find it very difficult being married to a black foreigner," she said, "but if that's your decision, what can I say? It's your life, not mine."

And so, we were married. A simple ceremony, performed by the Imam of the East London mosque, in the very same room that had welcomed me with its joss stick fragrance not so long ago. Mustafa wore his best suit, and I wore a printed silk sari, white with huge black flowers all over it, a white rose in my hair, no jewellery, and no make-up. I wanted to look the way I am. Plain and simple, nothing elaborate or artificial.

The day was 25th December. It was *Quaid-e-Azam* (Great Leader) Mohammad Ali Jinnah's birthday, the politician and barrister who fought singlehandedly for a separate land for the Muslims of British India. It was also Christmas Day. So, when Christians around the world celebrate the birth of Jesus Christ, and the people of Pakistan commemorate Quaid-e-Azam's birthday, we would have genuine reason to celebrate, too.

◦─◦◦◈◦◦─◦

Having completed his studies and secured a position as a computer design engineer in International Computers and Tabulators, Manchester, Mustafa bought a house in Cheshire. Sometime later, Mohammad followed. And although we settled down and started a family, I was well aware that this was not our forever home. The time would inevitably come when we would have to uproot and move to Pakistan. This was the promise Mustafa had made to his parents when they had expressed their fears that if he married a British girl he might never return.

When our third daughter, Biba, was born, Mustafa's father wrote an unusually long letter advising him to seriously consider returning home. You have three daughters now. How will you bring them up to be Muslims in an environment that is alien to Islamic culture, he had asked? Something that was preying on my mind, too. True, I had accepted Islam, but having so little knowledge how would I be able to guide my children?

Thereafter, our talks would often centre around life in Pakistan. While Mohammad, as always, did most of the talking and focussed on mundane but essential things, Mustafa felt the need to impress.

"You will have a wonderful life in Pakistan," he assured me. "You will have lots of saris." He knew I loved wearing a sari. "At least one hundred, as well as servants galore."

Mohammad tried his best to teach me Urdu. He bought a book, Teach Yourself Urdu, which he hoped would help, but it didn't.

"Look!" I said, slamming the book shut after the very first lesson. "I honestly can't see how this book is going to help me. I mean, *Mai Gujranwala ja rehi hai* (I am going to Gujranwala). Now, your homes are in Lahore. Right? So, why would I be going to Gujranwala? I need to learn simple but practical things like, where is the toilet? What is your name? Where are you going? or Where can I buy this or that?"

The lessons continued, though not regularly, and I made little progress. Perspicaciously, before embarking on our epic journey to Pakistan, Mustafa warned me not to make any attempt to speak Urdu without first consulting him. Wise words, indeed! If only I had heeded them.

A Jubilant Welcome

Suddenly, there was a lot of noise in my ears, and they were hurting me. I opened my eyes to find Bubbles standing between my knees, crying, and pressing her hands against her ears. Mustafa, one arm holding little Biba, the other guiding Jimmy, was shuffling along the aisle, and Beenish, bless her, was sitting upright in her seat but fast asleep. It took me a few moments to realise where I was.

We were nearing the end of our journey and the plane was slowly descending, which explained the pressure in our ears. I held bubbles close and rocked her, whispering assurances that her earache would soon get better. Finally, our plane landed. We had arrived in Karachi, Pakistan.

As we clambered down the stairs, frantically juggling children with hand luggage, we were suddenly faced with a sea of oddly dressed people, some waving and singing excitedly, others clutching garlands of pink and orange flowers, surging forward to meet and greet us. Mohammad had told me Pakistani people were very friendly and welcoming, but I had never imagined a welcome like this.

Mustafa noticed the look of wonderment on my face and smiled. "These people are Bhutto supporters," he shouted, hoping to be heard above the noise of the slowing engines and the jubilant chanting and cheering of the crowd.

"Zulfikar Ali Bhutto, the Prime Minister. He was on our plane."

And I suddenly felt hot with embarrassment.

In the arrival lounge, however, I had my moment of fame. Mustafa's uncle and his wife, and Bhai Jan and his wife were there to greet us. They put garlands of flowers around our necks, and people kept staring at me as though I was a celebrity. On the plane, one man had asked me if I was a film star. I felt flattered and must admit my clothes – a sliver lurex trouser suit with a long, bright red scarf, and red Scholl sandals on my very white feet, were not what they were used to seeing and did make me stand out.

Luggage secured in the boot by willing porters, hopeful of a generous tip, we were bundled into uncle's car, which he apparently was going to drive, even though he had a false leg. A heavy, wooden leg, quite unlike today's nifty prostheses. Bhai Jan and his wife sat in the chauffeur-driven car behind.

The roads were wide and as we passed by spacious bungalows, some with gates wide open to reveal big gardens and tree-lined driveways, Mustafa's promise to buy a pony for Bubbles suddenly came to mind. His uncle, to whose house we were going, had earned a doctorate, his special subject of study being the famous poet, Muhammad Iqbal, and enjoyed a distinguished position as Director of Allama Iqbal Academy as well as all the accompanying perks. Mustafa had boasted they had a grand house and garden, so surely, I thought, they must own a donkey or two.

"Aunty!" I ventured, smiling affably. *"Tum gadha hai?"*

Her head jerked sideways, but the look on her face was not what I had expected. "Kia (What)?" she asked.

And like the simpleton I was, I repeated, *"Tum gadha hai?"*

"Mustafa!" she almost screamed. *"Mujai samaj nahin atti* (I don't understand). *Tumhari biwi kia kheti hai* (What does your wife say)?

Mustafa, with Biba bouncing happily on his lap was in the front passenger seat, chatting to his uncle nineteen to the dozen, something I had never seen him do before. He stopped abruptly, but before he could say anything, I hastened to clarify what I had said.

"I only asked her if she has a donkey," I said, struggling to understand what all the fuss was about.

"And what exactly did you say," he asked. So, I told him.

Mustafa let out a horrified gasp. "Didn't I warn you not to speak Urdu without asking me. *Tum gadha hai* means, *You are a donkey.* That's what you said to her."

After apologising several times, I remained silent for the rest of the journey. My face was hot, I could feel it, and I was burning inside, too. An embarrassing start indeed to my new life in Pakistan!

Uncle stopped the car at the gates of a grand, two storey house and hooted. The gatekeeper opened it, and as we drove slowly along the driveway several servants appeared, eager to greet their master and, as I learned later, the beautiful *memsahib* they had heard so much about.

Mohammad had often told me about the narrow streets, chaos and congestion on the roads, and the poor living conditions, but what I had seen so far did not reflect poverty and chaos. What I saw pleased and impressed me. I was on cloud nine. Pakistan was everything I had hoped it would be. But we were in Karachi, a vibrant city that embraced freedom and modern culture. Soon, I reminded myself, we would be in a different world. Lahore!

After a short but wonderful stay in Karachi, servants at our beck and call, treating us like royalty, we were back in the air flying to our ultimate destination, Lahore. No joyful welcome awaited us there; and while Bhai Jan was finding a taxi for us, his wife handed me a black, neatly folded bundle. *"Yeh-lo!* (take this)" she said. *"Aur pehano!* (and wear it)."

She was smiling, revealing rather crooked teeth that marred her otherwise beautiful face. Cherub lips, and fine, tapered brows that highlighted her dancing, almond-shaped eyes! And from the expression on her face, I felt she was perhaps mocking me, or waiting for a shock reaction. But I had already prepared myself to remain calm whatever the situation.

"*Shukaria* (thank you)," I said, trying to make out what she had given me.

Mustafa was quick to notice my puzzled look. "It's a burka, Layla," he said, unfolding it and helping me to put it on. A very long silky coat that almost touched the ground, and with it a head covering with two veils and long ribbon-like strips for tying under the chin.

"All women wear a burka. It's the custom here," he explained.

"Oh my days!" I gasped. "But Bhabi Ji (that's what I was advised to call Bhai Jan's wife) isn't wearing one."

"That's because she often accompanies Bhai Jan on his business trips to Karachi, and he doesn't mind if she goes without a burka. Karachi is a modern city. People there are more liberal and fashion conscious. But in Lahore nearly all women wear burkas."

"Do I really have to wear one?" I persisted. "I mean, look at me! I look ridiculous. I look like a nun."

"Well, that's the whole purpose of a burka. No woman looks attractive in it, and that's why others, especially men, tend not to bother her," was his candid reply.

"And the good thing is, you don't have to dress up to go anywhere. You could be wearing your pyjamas underneath the burka, and no one would be any the wiser. Anyway, I think it's best you wear it. My parents would be mortified if you didn't."

So, burka it was! Strange beginnings to a life that by any stretch of the imagination was more different than I could ever have foreseen. It was also beginning to dawn on me why Mohammad had been so unrelenting with his homilies about the more mundane aspects of Pakistani life. He was preparing me for the real Pakistan, not the one in my imagination or in my dreams.

Once, I did dream about Pakistan, after Mohammad had been explaining how very different life in Pakistan would be. The narrow, crowded streets, bustling crowds, and bizarre traffic! I dreamt I was being driven along a beautiful tree-lined avenue with grand houses on either side. So, I quietly smiled to myself as our taxi cruised along Mall Road, an avenue similar to the one I had seen in my dream.

I was thinking Mohammad must have been joking or exaggerating, just to test my resolve, but then we came to a busy intersection controlled by a traffic policeman. When it was our turn to move, we took a right turn, and there my dream was snatched away, to waft with the falling autumn leaves of the trees we had just left behind on Mall Road.

We were now heading for the walled city, the historic and cultural heart of Lahore, where Mustafa's family lived, and where he and all his siblings were born and brought up. The road narrowed and we had to slow down because of all manner of vehicles jamming the way, as well as pedestrians weaving recklessly in between, trying to cross over.

The children were so overcome with all the travelling and strange happenings to be their usual energetic selves and had slept longer and more frequently than usual. They were also unaccustomed to the heat. The noisy traffic, however, soon jerked them into wide-eyed alertness.

"Mummy! Daddy! Look at that man with a ladder!" shouted Jimmy, excitedly pointing to a Vespa motorbike, winding its way through the traffic, the pillion rider holding tightly on to the longest and oddest ladder I had ever seen. A few minutes later, another Vespa overtook us. Incredibly, the pillion rider was holding an upright tree. A real tree with branches, leaves, roots, and all. There seemed to be no limit, no restriction to what people could transport on a motorcycle.

As we slowly moved forward, several motorbikes passed us by loaded, it seems, with an entire family. Two or more little ones squeezed in front of the rider, presumably the Dad, and his burka-clad wife sitting precariously sideways behind him, one hand holding onto him, the other clutching yet another child.

It was like a circus. Rickety trucks, bullock carts, motorbikes, wagons, and rickshaws! And there were *tongas* too, horse-drawn carriages with two enormous wooden-spoked wheels. There were also the donkeys Mustafa had boasted about. Not the seaside donkeys I was used to seeing, but thin, tired looking donkeys pulling carts, some overloaded with bricks or bizarre objects, others with fruit or vegetables.

"Look, Daddy!" said Bubbles, and I was afraid she had noticed the donkeys, too. But luckily, something else had caught her attention.

"What's that?" And she pointed to what looked like an enormous white shuttlecock, bobbing, and weaving in and out of the traffic.

"It's a woman," Mustafa replied. "And like mummy, she is wearing a burqa, but hers is a different style of burka."

"But how can she see?" Bubbles asked, the first of many questions that followed, which Mustafa tried his best to answer. Little wonder the children were befuddled. I was too, in this overwhelmingly weird new world.

The taxi stopped, and there stood Mustafa's house, three stories tall and wider than most houses we had passed. I was trying my best to look calm and composed despite the mix of emotions brewing inside me. All my life I had been used to seeing tree-lined streets with clean pavements, and houses with beautiful gardens, but before me were cement-walled dwellings and a dirt road that narrowed so that opposite houses were almost touching distance apart.

Immediately opposite was an open space where two cows were tied to a stake and an old woman was squatting, making cowpats from their dung, and throwing them onto the outer wall of her house.

The moment of truth! Mustafa had once shown me a picture of his mother and younger sister, but that was all. What about the rest of his family, I wondered? What were they like? And more importantly, would they like me?

I climbed the stairs, holding tightly onto little Biba for comfort and support. She was awake and bewildered, as were all the children. Only Mustafa seemed comparatively at ease. At the top of the stairs, everyone had gathered to greet the hero son, and the British bride he had boasted about in his letters.

My burka enthused gasps of appreciation from the women folk, and Mustafa's father was surprisingly generous with his welcome, singing my praises and saying, *"bohat acchi"* (very good) and *"bohat khoobsurat"* (very beautiful). However, from the look on my mother-in-law's face, I guessed she didn't appreciate his spontaneous compliments.

Emotions were now running riot inside my pounding chest. The straps of my veiled headwear were beginning to choke me. I was sweating too, and, not surprisingly, desperately in need of the loo.

"Where is the toilet?" I asked Mustafa, which was one of the phrases I should have learnt in my Urdu lessons with Mohammad, instead of *Mey Gujranwala ja rehi hai* (I am going to Gujranwala).

Mustafa's youngest sister, my *nund*, (Urdu word for one's husband's sister) overheard and led me up a flight of stairs, across the roof to a brick hut with a corrugated tin roof. I unbolted the door and stepped inside. There was no wash basin, no sign of a toilet roll, and as far as I could see, no toilet. The only thing I recognised was a cistern attached to the wall. Oh my days! I said to myself, stepping back outside.

Luckily, Mustafa's sister was a college student and could speak English quite well. "What's wrong?" she asked.

"Where's the toilet. There's just a hole in the floor," I replied.

She stared at me quizzically, not understanding my concern. For her, I later learned, this was a modern toilet so why wasn't I pleased? What was my problem?

"Yes, there is," she said, opening the door wide. "There!" And she pointed to the hole. It was surrounded by white tiles. On the wall beside it was a small tap, and beneath it a *lota*, a plastic pot with a spout but no handle for cleaning oneself.

I was still confused. "But there's no seat. Nothing to sit on."

Having never been camping and 'roughed it' or been anywhere where there was no proper toilet, I was beginning to feel quite frustrated; and my poor *nund*, who had never seen a western style toilet, was completely baffled. "You don't sit, you squat." And she bent down to demonstrate.

Back downstairs again, my *nund* left me alone to face my mother-in-law and *dewarani* (Mustafa's younger brother's wife). I felt alone and defenceless. Where was Mustafa? Where were the children? And where was little Biba? I had entrusted her to my mother-in-law who was now sitting cross-legged on a *palang* (Asian-style bed), her oversized shawl draped over her head and most of her body.

"Biba?" I asked. "Where is Biba?"

My mother-in-law lifted her shawl and there, fast asleep and sweating from the warmth of her generous bosoms, was little Biba. Suddenly, totally overwhelmed by all the events of the day, I burst into tears. From the expression on all their faces, it was obvious they were at a loss to understand what had upset me. What was there to cry about? Especially as they had gone to great lengths to make us comfortable.

At last! Mustafa, who had been out meeting relatives, returned with the children and the evening meal was served. Lamb *biryani*, lamb *korma*, *shami kebabs* and *raita*, followed by *gajrela*, a seasonal sweet dish akin to rice pudding, made from grated carrots, sugar, rice, and milk, and garnished with chopped pistachio nuts, which became one of my favourite desserts. Dinner over, we were shown to our rooms and left alone to settle in.

The last of the three rooms had been set as a bedroom with two large *palang* placed side by side, dark brown built-in cupboards either side. No carpet, no rug, just a plain concrete floor. With their brightly coloured quilts, though, the beds were a welcome sight. It had been a very long day. By now, the children were exhausted. I was, too, but more mentally than physically.

So many questions were still unanswered. Where was the kitchen, the bathroom, and all the servants Mustafa had promised? What if the children needed the toilet in the middle of the night? But all that must wait till tomorrow, a new day that would surely bring renewed energy and resolve.

House of Doors

Dawn the next day was like nothing I had ever experienced or could have imagined or dreamt about. It was still dark when the silence of the night was interrupted by the *adhan* (call to prayer) from the nearby mosque, followed in succession by all the mosques around.

It was like a super dawn chorus in a British woodland, all the mosques calling out in harmony, and there was one distant call that deeply moved me. The muezzin had a pure, mellifluous voice that could only arise from the purest of souls.

When adhan was over, Mustafa and I got up to pray. "You go to the toilet first, if you need to," he said, "and I'll keep an eye on the children."

When I returned, Mustafa was waiting for me. "This is the *hamam*," he said, pointing to a huge, round container behind the door of the first room. "It's full of water, so you can do wudhu here."

The hamam had a lid with two handles, equal distance apart. In the lid itself was a circular hole about the size of a very small saucer with a hinged lid that could be opened to allow water to flow into the hamam from the tap directly above. And near the base of the hamam was a simple, on-off tap.

We had just finished saying our prayers when the sound of someone reciting the Quran drifted into our room. Beautiful, tuneful incantations as soulful as the distant call to prayer. I thought it must be the radio. It was, I later learnt, my father-in-law.

A simple, humble, and extremely hardworking man, he was punctual with his prayers, which he always said in the nearby mosque. After the morning prayer, he would read the Holy Book before going to the *bazaar* (market) to get breakfast for everyone. In this house, he was always the first one up. In the adjoining house, newly built for Bhai Jan and his growing family, it was Bhai Jan who got everyone out of bed before dawn.

We were waiting for Mustafa's father to return with our breakfast when there was a knock on the balcony door. It was Bhai Jan. He had climbed over from his balcony onto ours to do his morning round, greeting everyone, something he did every day before heading off to work. If Mustafa's father was the patriarch, honest, practical, and dependable, Bhai Jan was the indisputable cheerleader and the beating heart of this big family.

Time to explore the house! Where was the kitchen, I wanted to know? And the bathroom, and the servants? Where were they?

Behind the plain façade, the house was an odd u-shape in design. On the ground floor, there were three rooms either side with a large courtyard in the middle. A disappointingly insipid one. No fountain! No greenery whatsoever, not even a potted plant! Just a plain floor with an open gutter alongside the walls.

At the far end, opposite the entrance, were two doors side by side that I thought might be storerooms, and on the outer side of each was a winding staircase leading to the first floor, which was virtually a replica of downstairs. Three rooms each side, but with an additional smaller room built over the front entrance, and another even smaller room built on the landing of the two sets of stairs and overlooking the courtyard below.

Ours were the three rooms along the left side of the first floor – the right side when looking at the house from the outside. Two of the three rooms on the opposite side were home to *Bhayan* (which is what Mustafa called his younger brother) and his small family. The last room on that side belonged to *Abba Ji* (my father-in-law), *Ammi Ji* (my mother-in-law) and my *nund*, as did the room in the middle.

From the first storey, two sets of stairs continued up to the roof, a vast, oddly shaped space with walls on four sides – one that separated our house from Bhai Jan's, one overlooking the street, one overlooking a shed that housed milking buffalos and a place where the milk was made into pure *desi ghee* (butter oil), and another that overlooked a small mosque. In the centre, was a rectangular wall, similar to that on the first storey and overlooking the courtyard. On one side, next to Bhai Jan's house, was a small room, and even more stairs leading to the roof above it. On the other side, the mosque side, was a lean-to called a *barsati*.

And there was the toilet! It had been recently built for our benefit, so I wondered how they managed before. Later, when my nund told me, I wished I hadn't asked. The previous toilet, she explained, was a raised concrete slab with two holes to squat over, enabling two people to sit together side by side and chat while they did their business.

Every day, a cleaner would come and scoop the waste into a large *karahi* (shallow metal dish) using a *jharu* (bundle of twigs tied together) and then, skilfully balancing it on the head, carry it away, to dump into the open sewer that slowly wound its way throughout the walled city. Where it ended up, I never dared to ask.

Thankfully, Pakistan's modern towns and cities have proper sewerage systems and even, in some cities, underground electric cables. The old walled city had neither. Water from the houses, including the toilets, was simply flushed into the open gutters outside, ending up in the open sewer. Unsightly pylons blighted every street, dangling cables criss-crossing their way like tangled serpents to all the houses in the vicinity.

Back to our new home!

Three good sized interconnected rooms, ending with a balcony overlooking the street, just wide enough to stand in, but no space for chairs or potted plants. The middle room was obviously the sitting room. It had two built-in cupboards, a three-piece sofa set with fabric cushioning and polished, solid wood armrests. And like all the rooms, a plain concrete floor bereft of rugs or carpets. But what this room lacked in décor it made up for in doors.

Two sets of double doors led to the bedroom. Three sets of double doors led to the open corridor outside that overlooked the courtyard, and two more sets of double doors led to the first room, the one with the hamam. In all three stories, there were no less than fifty-one double doors, and seven single doors, each one made of solid wood. House of Doors! That's what I called it. But not a single window. Only *roshandans*, small windows close to the ceiling used as skylights in winter and opened for ventilation in summer to allow the rising hot air to escape.

"This is the kitchen," said Mustafa. It was the room with the hamam.

"Oh my days!" I gasped, as taken aback as I had been with the toilet. "But how can you call this a kitchen?" I questioned. "Where is the sink, the oven, the worktops? And what about kitchen cupboards for dishes and foodstuff? And where's the fridge?"

It soon became apparent that there were none. There were cupboards built into the walls, just like the ones in the other two rooms, five in total, all painted very dark brown.

But if I was unhappy with my big kitchen, empty as it was, I was even more shocked to see my mother-in-law's. Immediately opposite mine, it was the room built on the landing, overlooking the courtyard. It was so small it could only accommodate a fireplace, a couple of *piries* (low stools) and an *ungeethi*, which basically was a metal bucket with a grill over the top on which to rest a cooking pot or tawa, and near the base, a hole for the wood fire that fuelled it.

Built into the wall on the courtyard side, there was also a cupboard with several shelves, and wire mesh back and doors that allowed light to enter the otherwise dingy room. And that was it! And because there was no water supply in her mini kitchen, our so-called kitchen was always open so she could take water from the hamam whenever she needed.

I had braced myself for all kinds of challenges, but the enormity of the move to Pakistan began to weigh heavily upon me. Nothing met my expectations, and I wondered where I had I landed myself. Once again, I knew the answer. The place of no return! Like Hernan Cortes when he set off to conquer the Aztec Empire! As a signal to his men that there was no turning back, he destroyed all his boats.

For them, it was win and survive or be defeated and die.

For me, it was to accept, adjust, and learn to thrive. I should have paid more attention each time Mohammad briefed me on the mundane aspects of life in Lahore but, idealistic, irresponsible neophyte that I was, I wore rose tinted spectacles and chose not to see or hear.

I suddenly realised none of us had had a bath since our stay in Karachi. Even there, they had what I considered rather antiquated bathrooms, no bathtub but overhead showers that showed signs of rust. At least they were bathrooms! Dare I ask where the bathroom was here, if indeed there was one?

Well, as it turned out, there was a bathroom. Downstairs! What I first thought was an understairs cupboard. It was small and as basic as the kitchen. There was a hand basin with two taps, but only the cold one worked, and a pipe beneath it that drained the water directly onto the floor. Under the sloping roof was another tap, again cold water only, and beneath it a large plastic tub and *donga* (a large mug for scooping up water to pour over one's body).

Worse still, as I was soon to discover, there was running water only twice a day, early morning, and afternoon. And even worse than that was the fact that nearly all the downstairs rooms were rented out as *gudaams* (storage space for wholesale goods). So, by far the biggest challenge for me was how to get in and out of the bathroom without being seen by the men who would come and go without warning to store or collect their merchandise.

For the next few days, the house was buzzing with visitors, all eager to see the new *memsahib*, which was embarrassing as well as uncomfortable. I felt like a new item on display in a shop window. They would stare and nod, and I would smile back like a Cheshire cat. It did not help that I barely understood a word they said. While some spoke rapid Punjabi, others spoke more clearly in Urdu, but most of the time I couldn't tell the difference.

We were into our second week in our new home when Mustafa told me his mother, whom I now addressed as *Ammi Ji* (*ammi* meaning mother, and *ji* a sign of respect), was going to take me to see Mohammad's mother while he stayed home to look after the children.

"Why can't Mohammad's mother come here?" I asked.

"She's not well," he replied. "I promised Mohammad you would meet her as soon as possible, and there are the gifts he sent for her, remember."

"But why can't you come with me? Why can't we all go?" I suggested, hoping he would agree. "I'm sure she must be waiting to see you, as well as the children."

"No, the children can't go," was his resolute reply. "It would be too difficult for them. No, you go, and I'll meet her some other time."

So, it was settled. Wearing burkas, faces covered by two veils, we set off with Ammi Ji leading the way. She was short, less than five feet tall, with a very heavy bosom, rounded figure and feet that must have been size three by standard UK shoe size. She had the advantage of knowing where she was going, but even then, considering her age and figure, she was amazingly nimble.

As she cleverly manoeuvred her way, avoiding gutters and potholes, weaving in and out, overtaking other pedestrians, I struggled to keep up with her. Not knowing which turn she would take next, I had to keep my eyes on her and at the same time remember to look down to avoid tripping over or stepping into the open gutters that lined the narrow streets.

Considering I had two veils restricting my vision, I thought I was doing quite well. But then Ammi Ji, now some distance ahead of me, stopped, turned, and looked back at me. *"Chuko, Layla, chuko!"* she said with an urgency in her voice.

"What's *chuko, chuko?"* I asked myself, repeating the words as I raced along, feeling annoyed with Ammi Ji for walking so fast and with myself for not knowing the meaning of the word, *chuko.* Since I was lagging, and she was walking so fast, I decided *chuko* must mean *quickly,* and tried to walk faster, but moments later I landed in a pothole and almost twisted my ankle.

And then, as if things could not get worse, we entered a very narrow street where the gutter ran through the middle, so I had to straddle my way across it or hop from one side to the other, while trying desperately to keep up. Ammi Ji looked back again. "Chuko!" she called out. "Chuko niqab!" It was then I noticed she had flung both veils over her head, and it suddenly dawned on me that *chuko* didn't mean *quickly,* but *lift,* and in this case it meant, lift the veil so you can see.

If only I had known, I would not have struggled so much. Anyway, I had learnt a new word. I had also learnt that when needs must, lift the veil. I also understood why Mustafa refused to send the children.

—◆—

Mohammad's house was nothing like ours. Ours was double-fronted, and despite my initial shock reaction at the lack of amenities, it was more spacious and grander than most. His house was so small, the area of a postage stamp in comparison I would say. Outside, a goat was tied up, and while we waited for someone to open the front door I had to keep moving to avoid being nibbled or butted.

The single door opened to reveal two inter-connected rooms and a narrow, winding staircase with very steep stone steps leading up to the first floor where there were two more rooms and a tiny balcony. Mustafa's mother was sitting on a *charpai*, a typical Asian bed with four chunky wooden legs and a woven jute centre part.

"Asalaamu-alaikum! (Peace be upon you!)" said Ammi Ji.

"Walaikum-us salaam! (Peace be upon you, too!)" Mohammad's mother responded, slipping her feet into her chappals, and standing up to greet her in the traditional Pakistani way, hugging and touching cheeks, first the right, then left, then right again. And then it was my turn. She was tall and well-built, and I noticed her hands and feet were very big for a woman. Her embrace was more like a bear hug and almost took my breath away, what was left of it after my challenging walk and the very steep stairs.

Despite her trojan-like appearance, she seemed a kind, gentle soul, and surprisingly soft spoken. And when she smiled, she revealed teeth like Mohammad's with a wide gap between the two front ones. She was genuinely pleased to see me and kept nodding approvingly, as if acknowledging that her son had done a very good job finding a wife for his best friend. Although she didn't look unwell, I later learned she had a serious illness (cancer perhaps?) and that good days alternated with difficult ones, forcing her to stay at home.

She sat cross-legged on her charpai, and we sat opposite her on very high, brightly coloured stools, set apart by a small table. Her daughter-in-law, to whom the downstair rooms belonged, then served us with tea, delicious ripe guava segments, plain cake, and my new favourite dessert, gaajar halwa. There was also a dish of delicious pine nuts that I had never seen or tasted before. And, like my visits to her son's house in England, I felt honoured and welcome.

Challenges Galore

In a way, we were beginning to settle down. At least, the children were. They were picking up new Urdu words every day, and their cousins were always ready and willing to entertain them. The main problem was me and how I was supposed to manage.

You will have servants galore, that's what Mustafa had told me, but where were they? So far, the only servants I had seen were two sweepers, young women who had come from their *gaoun* (village) to earn a living in the city. But they only came for a couple of hours every morning to clean the floors with *jharu* and *thupri* (broom made of twigs tied together and a wet cloth), squatting and rhythmically swaying with each sweeping motion, their *dupattas* (head coverings) and long dresses trailing along the floor behind them.

There was also Chacha, a man servant from the shop who came at midday to collect the tiffin tin containing Abba Ji's lunch, which usually consisted of curry and freshly made chapatis. Ammi Ji's chapatis never failed to puff up into a ball, something that always amazed me. She knew exactly when to put the lighted wood into the *ungeethi* and when to withdraw it to make the perfect chapati, or *roti* as she called it.

Wondering where the servants were, triggered a folk song I often used to sing: *Where Have All the Flowers Gone?* And partly because the tune kept going around in my head, and partly to cheer myself up, I started to sing, changing the words slightly to suit my present dilemma.

> Where have all the servants gone, long time
> passing?
> Where have all the servants gone, long
> time ago?
> Where have all the servants gone?
> Gone to gaoun everyone.
> When will they all return?"
> Oh when will they all return?

Mustafa was now standing beside me. "Where *are* all the servants," I asked, but there was no immediate answer.

"Well, actually, there aren't any right now, except the cleaning women," he sheepishly replied. "But I'll ask Ammi Ji about it."

"And what about the kitchen? We need a sink, and a worktop with drawers and cupboards. And it would be nice to have a breakfast table and chairs. Can you ask Ammi Ji, please?"

"I'll ask her," he promised.

True to his promise this time, Mustafa put the question of servants and kitchen improvements to his parents. Ammi Ji said she would arrange for someone to help me with the dishes and laundry. And Abba Ji agreed to call the carpenter to make a worktop. But a sink, he explained, would not be of much help because most of the time there was no running water. It came only briefly twice a day, which is why the hamam was there.

In the evenings, it was the custom in our new home for everyone to gather in Ammi and Abba Ji's room. Bhai Jan usually joined us, adding joviality to the general gossip with his jokes and anecdotes, but Bhabi Ji normally stayed at home. I guess she had had more than her share of family gatherings, and probably quarrels, too, and valued her new-found independence. Besides, she had six children to look after.

As we sat on *charpoys*, the main furniture in Abba Ji and Ammi Ji's room, we would eat *Kinu*, a hybrid variety of orange, or peanuts, or pine nuts, casually letting the peelings or shells fall to the floor to be swept up in the morning. There was something wholesome and sublime about huddling together on a cold winter evening, peeling fruit, shelling, munching nuts, not caring about the mess, and sharing jumbo size quilts to keep warm.

One evening, I was whispering something to Mustafa, in English of course, when I noticed Abba Ji was watching me, smiling, and nodding approvingly. He then turned to Ammi Ji.

"Dekho, Begum, kasai Layla pyaar aur tameez sai appnai miya kai saath baat kertai hay (See, misses, how Layla lovingly and politely talks to her husband)."

Ammi Ji's big eyes suddenly narrowed as though warning him to be careful. Pursing her lips, she then asked him, *"Aapko kesay patta hay woh kiya keh rehe hay?* (How do you know what she's saying?). *Aapko to angrezi samjh nahi aati* (You don't understand English). *Kiya patta woh appni zabaan mai usko gaaliya nikal rehe ho* (For all you know, she might be swearing at him in her own language)."

Everyone laughed, and I smiled, although I had no idea what they found so amusing. It was only when we were in our room that Mustafa explained the reason for all the laughter. It was hardly my fault, I argued, that Abba Ji seemed so enamoured by me.

Later, it occurred to me that he greeted others affectionately, too. He always referred to Bhayan's small son as *bohat accha* (very good), and every time he saw little Biba, he would say, *"Biba bohat acchi, bohat acchi* (Biba's very good, very good)."

That seemed to be his way with others, although not so towards his wife, at least not openly. There was a typical shyness customary among spouses in those days that prevented him from openly praising her, and I thought it rather sad. And perhaps it explained Mustafa's shyness, why he had so often passed messages to me through Mohammad. There are times, however, when we all welcome a little praise, even mild, harmless flattery, to restore our confidence and self-esteem.

Most mornings, when Abba Ji greeted Mustafa, he would say, *"Layla bohat acchi hay* (Layla is very good), *lekin woh namaz kai baad sojati hay* (but she goes to sleep after prayers)."

Abba Ji never slept after morning prayers, a habit I failed to emulate. I regularly said all five prayers, *Fajr, Zohr, Asr, Maghrib,* and *Isha,* and would often get up in the middle of the night to say *Tahajud,* the voluntary midnight prayer. But, despite Abba Ji's example and mild criticism, I struggled to stay awake after *Fajr,* which was very early in the morning, earlier still in summer. But I know I should have tried harder. Anyone who witnesses sunrise and experiences the quiet that follows dawn will advocate the habit of rising early every morning.

A week passed, and still no sign of the helper Ammi Ji had promised. The carpenter, however, was hard at work making the worktop, and he was good. It took him just a few days to complete the job. A Formica-covered working top, four low cupboards, each with two shelves, a huge drawer in between for cutlery and cooking utensils, and space below it for storing anything too large to fit in the cupboards.

In all honesty though, I felt it was small consolation for being without a sink or a cooking stove that would enable me to work standing. I was not used to squatting. It was difficult for me. Everything was. The toilet so far upstairs, the bathroom downstairs and of no use at all if the city's tube wells were switched off and the tub was empty.

The tub water was often freezing cold, and I had to brace myself before pouring the first donga-full over my body. The running tap water was just as cold, but I learned that if I let the water run for a minute or so, tepid water would follow.

I also learnt how to acclimatise myself to cold water, which was to first pour it over the knees until it felt warm, and then pour it slowly over the rest of the body, head last of all.

Once, I had just finished bathing and was about to open the door and run back upstairs when the gudaam men came. I waited with bated breath for a good half hour while they removed goods and loaded them onto a hand-drawn cart in the street outside. And to my horror, they left without closing the front doors, wide double doors, which made my escape even more embarrassing. And this became the new norm, struggling to plan bath time to coincide with water supply and at the same time avoid the gudaam men.

Now, if the hamam was the bane of my life, it was also my benefactor. Every morning, I had to open the small lid within the main lid to allow water from the tap above to fill the hamam, and then turn the tap off once it was full and close the lid, an exercise repeated in the afternoon. In between, we relied on the hamam for all the water we needed for drinking, washing hands and dishes, as well as for cooking.

One morning, I opened the lid and was reaching for the tap to turn it on when I saw a large furry hump perched on the u-bend of the pipe, and two bulging eyes staring back at me. It was a huge rat, frozen like a statue, hoping not to be seen. Not surprisingly, my screams frightened it away and brought Mustafa running into the kitchen to see what had happened.

"There was a huge rat sitting on the pipe," I told him, "But I don't know where it's gone. It could be anywhere. Look for it, please."

Mustafa searched every nook and cranny of the kitchen, but the furry intruder was nowhere to be found. "It must have run down the drainpipe," he said nonchalantly. "That's why it's important to keep the lid closed, to stop rats or mice or cockroaches from getting into the water."

Oh my days! What would I discover next? The children were already terrified of the cockroaches on the floor and creepy lizards on the walls, silently waiting to prey on the flies, mosquitoes, and other insects that settled within their reach. Should I now warn them about the vermin, too?

At the end of the day, I was usually exhausted, both mentally and physically. The children would fight to sleep next to me, but since little Biba always slept on my left side, I let the others take turns to sleep next to me on the right. In the darkness, where no one could see, bedtime was when I allowed my emotions to overflow. I would tell them stories I had made up about a naughty monkey who escaped from the zoo and found its way to school.

And then, recalling the repertoire of songs I had learnt over the years, I would sing: *My bonny lies over the ocean; There is not in this wide world a valley so sweet; Come Mister Tally Man, tally me banana; Someone's calling, kumbaya; In Dublin's fair city, where the girls are so pretty; Oh, the buzzing*

*of the bees in the cigarette trees; Puff, the magic dragon; Oh,
island in the sun;* and so many more.

Oblivious of the tears and my quivering, emotion-choked
voice, the children loved to listen, and invariably asked
me to sing a favourite song over and over again; and as I
sang, my mind would drift across land, sea and time to my
childhood home and the family I had left so far behind.
What were they doing? How were they? How many of them
were married? Did they have children? Did they miss me? I
certainly missed them.

I lost contact with my family after my marriage. "You
will not survive in Pakistan if your heart is in two places,"
Mohammad had advised me, so over time I allowed the
distance to become ever wider.

Ruth kept in touch, though. Her cheerful letters were
something to look forward to, and occasionally she would
send gifts for the children. Story books, jig-saw puzzles, and
laces and braiding for the frocks I sewed for the girls. I felt
blessed to have the solace of a life-long friend like her, despite
the distance between us and the fact that I could never tell
her what I was really going through. Lasting friendships are
priceless, like finding a pearl among the shingle.

<hr />

It was when the children were asleep that I had time to reflect
and re-energise myself to face the coming day with renewed
confidence and resolve. And sometimes, I would tip-toe
into the sitting room and write a poem or prose expressing

my anxiety or optimism, depending on inspiration and my current mood and circumstances.

Today! is a poem I wrote during such moments, to persuade myself to count my blessings, make the most of each day, and not worry about the future – a cathartic exercise like most of my poems.

Today!

Forget the shadows of the past, the laughter
and the sorrow,
For the past does not exist, neither does
tomorrow.
The past is buried deep in the scrolls of
history,
And tomorrow's far away, across a bridge
we cannot see.
But today is ours, my friend, today's a
certainty.
So live, enjoy; forget the fears and tears,
Embrace the precious moments; make each
moment last for years.
Today, is everything, my friend; make your
footsteps stretch for miles.
Don't let the seconds fade away but light
them up with smiles.
Live bravely and cheerfully, count the
blessings not the trials.

Finally, my helper arrived in the form of Chachi, Abu Ji's man servant's wife. Both had a tragic story to tell. During partition of India in 1947, when an estimated two million people were butchered in racial riots, Muslims and Hindus had to choose where to live, in Hindu majority India, or the new Muslim state of Pakistan.

Being Muslims in a predominantly Hindu region of India, Chacha's life and the lives of his wife and little children were in constant danger. So, they abandoned their home, farmland, cattle, and all their possessions and fled to Pakistan.

Once *Rajah* and *Rani* (king and queen) of lands that stretched as far as the eye could see, they became paupers overnight, fleeing with just a few small bundles of clothes and whatever food they could carry to sustain them during the long and perilous trek to Pakistan.

Exhausted, and destitute, they arrived in Lahore. But battered and bruised by the carnage that prevailed after partition, the ravaged city of Lahore had little to offer them. Both India and Pakistan were languishing from the aftermath of the most barbaric and unprecedented conflict, the atrocities of which, some claim, were even worse than those committed by the Nazis in World War II.

Mustafa was a schoolboy at the time and had witnessed several such attacks, although he could not bring himself to talk about it in any detail. His parents must have seen much, much more, but not once did they speak of it.

Many people, like Chacha and Chachi, would relate some story or other, but none of them gave any specifics of the trauma they had faced – the panic, the fear, and what they had seen. Whatever they suffered or witnessed must have been too painful to recall. And some buried the memories so deep, perhaps in an effort to persuade themselves that nothing had ever happened.

There was one question, however, that completely baffled everyone. How and why did it happen? Hindus, Muslims, and Sikhs had lived in harmony for ages, but almost overnight the devil turned men into demons, life-long friends into enemies. Your next-door neighbour, if his religion was not the same as yours, became your foe, crazed with hatred, revenge and … only God knows what. And only God knows what caused minds to flip from human-being to beast.

In fear and desperation, people fled for their lives, some carrying infants or dragging little ones along. But many did not make it to safety. Thousands were slaughtered or burned alive in their homes; others fell victim to the maniac mobs on the streets.

Despite their ordeal and misfortune, Chacha and Chachi were pure-hearted souls with the attributes of a true Muslim – humility, gratitude, kindness, fortitude, and the patience of *Yaqub* (Job). There was no bitterness and never a harsh word. I felt truly honoured to know them. They humbled me.

Chachi came each morning and stayed till midday. After washing the dishes at the hamam, she would take the clothes downstairs and wash them in the bathroom, scrubbing them with a huge chunk of washing soap, banging the dirty suds out with a *dunda*, a heavy wooden club, and then rinsing them in the tub.

Balancing the washed clothes in a large *karahi* on her head, she would slowly climb the two flights of stairs to the roof where I had fixed two washing lines, and where clothes dried easily in the midday sun. And while she hung the clothes, I prepared lunch for her, usually a curry dish cooked by yours truly, and chapatis from the bazaar, for I had yet to master the art of making them myself. She would eat slowly, savouring each morsel, thanking Allah, and blessing me. And I would look on in awe and admiration, thinking she was the one who deserved all the blessings.

Cooking was yet another challenge for me. My stove, though better than Ammi Ji's wood-burning ungeethi, was a kerosene stove, akin to ones used for camping. Using it was one thing but maintaining it in good working condition was another, refilling it with kerosene oil when the bottom container part ran dry, and rethreading the strands of cotton wicks when they had burnt through. And because the stove rested on the floor, I had to squat on a low stool to cook. Silently, I cursed the stove, as well as the hamam.

But then one morning, I sat down to fill a pan with water to make tea and noticed the hamam was leaking. I removed the big lid to look inside and discovered a hole about the size of a small coin in the base. There was a lot of rust debris on the bottom, too. What to do? How to stop the leak before all the precious water trickled down the drain, leaving us with an empty hamam?

And then I had a brainwave. Chewing gum is sticky, I thought, and I had some hidden away. So, I popped several pieces into my mouth and chewed it until it was soft and pliable. I rinsed it under the tap to clean my spit away before placing it over the hole on the underside of the base. I then sat and watched, stroking the hamam as though apologising for the countless times I had cursed it, waiting for any signs of a leak, and at the same time praying the chewing gum would hold fast. And it did, for several days until it could be repaired.

Was I glad when the hamam finally had a shiny new bottom! It made me count my blessings.

Changing Seasons

Time flew by! Winter, with its sunny days and cold nights had been supplanted by spring, a short but pleasant season of the year. Bubbles now went to a credited English medium school, and Jimmy had been registered for admission later on. My thoughts were now focussed on Mustafa. Wasn't he supposed to be looking for a job?

Since our arrival in Lahore, he had changed in so many ways. The Mustafa I married wore a shirt and tie for work, smart trousers, polished shoes, and a tailored tweed jacket I loved the smell of. He now wore shalwar kameez whenever he went outside and, to my horror, a *dhoti* at home – a long piece of cloth wrapped around the waist and secured by overlapping the ends and tucking them inside.

Even worse, he had resigned himself to the fact that he would never find a job conducive to his qualifications and experience as a computer design engineer. But we knew that before we embarked on this journey, I argued. We knew computers were virtually unheard of in Pakistan. He should at least try for the next best thing. But he seemed content to tag along with his father and work in the shop, even though Abba Ji had told him he didn't need his help.

So, I started to search for a job for him, scrutinising the classified pages of the Pakistan Times. Reading the newspaper was interesting, and I would often find humour where it was not intended, like a brief report saying, "The policeman caught the man with a donkey." And in my mind, I tried to imagine how he did that. Did he throw the donkey at the man to stop him running away, or what?

I also found respite reading the newspaper. It helped to remind me there was a world outside this House of Doors, and that I was still a part of it. There were several job vacancies I thought Mustafa might be interested in, but he wasn't. And I sort of understood why. He had given up a prestigious job and all the comforts of life in England to be with his ailing father, but he was neither given the financial support nor the welcome he expected. Moreover, he could never hope for a job like the one he had left behind. How it must have hurt him!

Relatives would come and say to me, "You are *Jannati*," meaning I would go to Heaven. That, they explained, was because I had sacrificed my home and family to become a Muslim. It made me feel very uncomfortable. Only God knows who will go to Heaven. And if I had become a Muslim, it was not through any sacrifice I had made. Mustafa was the one who had sacrificed. I was a mother and housewife in England, and still was. My status had not changed, but Mustafa's had. He had been part of an elite team of engineers. He had his own house and car. Here, he had virtually nothing.

Even so, I was at a loss to understand why he did not search for a job. When needs must, any decent job would do. He had no business training or experience, so why was he content to work in Abba Ji's shop. Moreover, it was in the noisy, crowded, chaotic heart of the wholesale market, so unlike his quiet office in Manchester.

How could he toss aside all that hard work earning a degree, not to mention the money his father had spent on him? Some family members were beginning to doubt he had a degree at all. But that is how it was and how it continued to be. No real job, except for working with his father and Bhai Jan, oftentimes not working at all. It was as though he had given up before even trying.

But if there was one thing Mustafa never gave up on, it was prayer. And we were fortunate. Throughout the day, the melodic call from all the minarets would echo around the city, reminding us it was time to pray. And that is why, despite the privation and all the things I cursed, I loved Lahore. It was a crazy, captivating city with a beating heart and soul.

⸺⸻❈⸻⸺

When we first arrived, it had surprised me how well Abba Ji was. He did not look like a man with a serious heart condition. Gradually, however, there were tell-tale signs that his health was failing. He would climb the stairs more slowly, and after Jumma prayers on Friday, his only day off from work, he would spend the afternoon sleeping. A hardworking man if ever there was one, there was a time when he literally worked day and night. In the daytime, he would be in his shop. At night, he would work the night shift on the railway.

By mid-April, it was very hot. But if the days were becoming unbearable, the nights offered little relief. The cement-plastered walls trapped the sun's heat, making the rooms stifling hot. Opening all the roshandans made little if any difference, so Abba Ji decided it was time to retreat to the roof to sleep.

While the male members of the family now walked around half naked, dhotis draped around the lower half of their bodies, the women wore thin cotton shalwar kameez (kurta and baggy trousers). I needed new clothes. Urgently! The clothes I had brought with me were unsuitable for this unbearably hot weather. The children needed new clothes, too, so I asked Mustafa if we could go shopping.

"Where can I buy shalwar kameez?" I asked, and then, out of the blue, I remembered his promise to buy me lots of saris.

In England, during the daytime, I would wear slacks and a baggy jumper, but come evening, when all the chores were done and the children were asleep, I would often change into a sari. It was my favourite dress, and Mustafa once promised that in Pakistan he would buy lots of beautiful saris for me. At least one hundred! That's what he said. But, like the pony and the servants he promised, there weren't any.

Despite the disappointment, I persuaded myself that it was probably just as well. When all the other women were wearing shalwar kameez, I would look completely out of place wearing a sari. It was also some consolation that when I tried to imagine myself sitting down by the hamam or the oil stove or running up and down the stairs dressed in a sari, I just couldn't. It was simply not practical.

The sari was a dress to be worn on special occasions like weddings, and it was popular in some regions, worn particularly by women in Karachi, but it was not commonly worn in Lahore, and definitely not in our House of Doors.

"You can't actually buy shalwar kameez," Mustafa finally answered. "Not ready made. You have to buy material and then sew them."

My mind flashed back to those missionary meetings of my childhood, sewing frocks for children in foreign lands. I had a sewing machine and could cut out and sew simple frocks for the girls, but I never thought I would have to sew my own clothes as well.

"Of course, you won't have to sew them yourself," Mustafa assured me. "You buy the material and then take it to the tailor master. He sews everyone's clothes. Ask Ammi Ji or Bhayan's wife. They will take you there."

What a relief! And a trip to the bazaar, tailor master, too! That should be interesting, I thought. So, the very next day, burka clad, I set off with my daewarani for the nearby market. I had learnt to drape the inner veil over the lower part of my face, leaving the eyes uncovered, allowing the outer veil to fully cover my face. In this way, my face was still hidden, but with only one veil over the eyes I could see much better.

Despite the burka and the veils, people in the bazaar tended to stare at me. Some even recognised that I was a foreigner because they called out, *"Memsahib, aou, deko* (Madam, come and see)," inviting me to see the wares they had to offer; and several times I was pestered by beggars. Because they sat on the ground, the beggars could see my feet, which my chappals barely covered. And then I understood that it was my uncovered hands and feet that gave my ethnicity away.

Everywhere was crowded, and at the cloth shop I tried to keep a low profile by keeping my hands under my veils and letting my daewarani do all the talking, not that I would have been able to anyway. Yards and yards of printed, fine cotton material were rolled out for our approval, all so beautiful it was difficult to choose.

Having purchased materials for several suits, we started back home, stopping on the way at the *bartan wallah* (crockery shop) where I bought several plates and dishes for the kitchen, all very cheap. We reached home, loaded with our purchases, feeling very pleased, and already planning our trip to the tailor master's shop, but it was not close by, in fact a tonga ride away, so it would have to wait for another day.

❖

The summer exodus to the roof began. The *barsati* housed all the charpoys, protecting them from the weather. In winter, they would be carried or dragged out for everyone to sit on, to soak up and enjoy the warm sunshine. Daytime in winter was spent mostly on the roof. The children would play, while the women prepared whatever meal was on the menu, shelling peas, chopping vegetables, pounding spices into fine powder, or ginger and garlic into paste.

When Mustafa's married sisters visited, which was often because they also lived within the walled city, there were all manner of activities on the roof. There was even alfresco dining, Pakistani style. Ammi Ji would carry her ungeethi upstairs and cook *saalan* (curry) and *rotis* with her usual expertise.

Infants would run naked in the wide-open space, swinging their arms, kicking the air, playing with nothing but sticks or fresh vegetable peelings, enjoying the freedom and the sun on their little brown bodies. When it was bath time, oh my, did they have a scrubbing! Smothered from head to toe with lifebuoy soap, some would cry their soapy eyes out, while others, knowing there was no escape, bore the scrubbing in silent submission.

Asr prayer time signalled the exodus from the roof, where life downstairs would resume as normal. Now, however, it was time for a reversal of routine. Days were spent downstairs, all fans turning full-speed, and in the evening, after *Maghrib* prayers, everyone would make their way upstairs, clutching pillows, sheets, quilts, jugs of water, and whatever else was needed for the night. Each would then take their charpai from the barsati, either dragging it or carrying it on their back, to their assigned space. And that is where we all slept. Beneath the open sky!

It was June, and the daily temperature had now risen to around 38 degrees centigrade. Apart from the unbearable heat, I was suffering from prickly heat, and my entire body was covered in a rash of tiny red spots that were infuriatingly itchy. No one else had it. Only me. And I wasn't sure what to do because I had never had it before. I used a comb to scratch myself, which only exacerbated the itching. I tried applying calamine lotion, but it did little to help. And then my nund gave me some prickly heat powder, which brought some relief.

"The rash will disappear when the monsoon rains come," she said.

"When will that be," I asked, hoping she would say any time soon.

"About the end of July," she casually replied.

Mustafa did not like the heat at all but kept himself cool by taking a bath as often as he could. In the winter everyone would avoid having a bath because the water was so cold, but now, when we all craved a cold shower, the water was teasingly warm, having come through pipes exposed to the scorching sun.

Before the arrival of the annual monsoon rains, dust storms, known as *andhi*, were a common occurrence. At the first sign of the whirling, dust laden winds, we would frantically gather our bedding and abandon the roof, but by the time we reached our rooms they were already covered by thick layers of dust.

Laboriously, we would clean up the mess, only to experience another dust storm a few days later. And then another. I hated the dust. In England I used to dust about once a week, if that, but here dusting was a daily chore. Nothing was without drama, it seemed, in this city of endless wonders.

Very late one evening, lying on my charpai with little Biba beside me, I became aware that something was going on the other side of the roof where Ammi and Abba Ji slept. I stood up and saw that Mustafa and everyone else had gathered around Abba Ji's charpai, so I went over to see what was happening.

Bhai Jhan was helping Abba Ji into a sitting position, but Abba Ji groaned and motioned that he wanted to lie down again. Bhai Jan then gently pressed his forehead while Mustafa and Bhayan pressed his legs, and Ammi Ji and my nund pressed his arms, a common practice when someone was aching from sickness or fatigue, usually much appreciated. But not this time! Abba Ji was clearly in considerable pain or discomfort.

As the night progressed, Abba Ji's pain worsened, his condition serious, so Bhai Jan rushed off to look for a taxi to take him to the hospital. Meanwhile, Mustafa and Bhayan helped him down the two flights of stairs, across the courtyard to the front doorway. The taxi arrived, and I watched from the roof as they all helped Abba Ji onto the back seat. And as I looked down, a quiet voice inside was telling me I would not see him again.

Two days later, we were all on the roof, including Bhabi Ji who was generally absent from family gatherings, when Bhai Jan returned from the hospital. And as he appeared in the doorway at the top of the stairs, all eyes were on him, eager to know how Abba Ji was. Bhai Jan stood silent for a moment and then burst into tears.

"Abba Ji's gone," he sobbed, his chest and shoulders heaving uncontrollably. Abba Ji had suffered a massive heart attack and died.

Bhai Jan's wife came and put an arm around him and led him, still sobbing, to where Ammi Ji was sitting, her lips pursed to stifle any outpouring of grief, her big eyes welling with tears. It's true to say a part of everyone died that night. There was now a gaping void in the family that no one could fill.

"I'm glad we came," I whispered to Mustafa later that day. "So glad we were able to spend some time with him." Mustafa nodded. It was small consolation, but he agreed.

Abba Ji's body arrived from the hospital, but before the women could see him, he was given the ritual bath, which took place in the courtyard below close to the bathroom. A makeshift canopy shielded him from being seen from above, but no one would have dared to look down anyway. A dead body was treated with the greatest dignity and respect, especially by family members.

After bathing, the body was wrapped in a white cotton shroud – the very shroud Abba Ji had taken with him to *Hajj*, the pilgrimage to Mecca, to wash and purify in *Zam Zam*, water from the sacred well. He had then packed it away in a trunk for use on this very day.

Only when the bathing rituals were over were we allowed to see him. I was scared. I had never seen a dead person before. Neither had the children, and because they were far too young to understand they were kept away. Abba Ji looked asleep, except that his face was ashen grey. But what did I expect, I asked myself? It was only the beating of the heart and circulation of blood throughout the body that brought colour to the skin. His life was over, a sad reality that would take us all a long time to come to terms with.

As word of Abba Ji's death spread, neighbours, friends, and relatives from inside the city and beyond began to arrive. Ammi Ji's room, the biggest in the house, had all the furniture removed and rugs, specially hired for the occasion, were spread over the floor for the women to sit on. Men sat separately, some in Bhayan's room, others in the courtyard below.

Abba Ji's body now lay on a cot in the centre of the courtyard, allowing all who entered to pay their respects and offer a prayer. His shrouded, camphor-scented body had been covered with a green cloth embroidered with Quranic verses and sprinkled with fresh rose petals. Finally, funeral prayers were said, and the men lifted the cot and carried it to the graveyard, reciting *Kalima Shahadat*. There, the body was buried, head facing Qibla. No coffin. Just a shroud.

The women paid their respects to Ammi Ji, trying their best to console her, and offering prayers that God may pardon the deceased. Prayers and reading verses of the Quran continued in the days that followed, and there was a constant stream of visitors, all eager to share Ammi Ji's grief and help her through the saddest of times.

It was a tradition that helped the grieving to come to terms with their loss and to focus on life once more. They would talk about Abba Ji until they could find nothing else to say. And there was never a bad word said about him, only praise for a man who had lived an honest, simple life. All prayed that he would be blessed with a place in Paradise.

Here was a family system like many others around the world where young and old lived under the same roof. Although there were a few charitable institutions for the homeless and destitute, there were no retirement homes as such. Old people were taken care of by the family, by their sons and their respective families. When the daughters married, they would leave home, but the boys usually remained with their parents even after marriage.

Households were therefore large and cohesive, everyone benefitting in various ways. Although the elders did not always appreciate their daughters-in-law, and vice versa, the children had the advantage of having several cousins to play with as well as their own siblings. It was a symbiotic family system. At times, chaotic and problematic, but one that generally worked well.

The Point of No Return

Mustafa had been seriously contemplating going back to England. He had not resigned from ICL but taken long leave on the understanding he could re-join his team any time. The children and I would stay behind until he found a job and a place to live, and then we would follow. That was the plan. He had even bought the plane ticket. But with his father's death, his plans were also laid to rest. With a heavy heart, he returned the ticket and claimed the refund. It was his mother who needed him now.

So, life went on, without Abba Ji's huge presence. Also, without Bhai Jan's rousing joviality to keep us going. He had been badly shaken by his father's death. All their lives they had lived together, and all his adult life Bhai Jan had worked alongside his father. For days, there was a dark cloud over our house, but it was the clouds in the sky that jerked us all back to normality.

The Monsoon had arrived. And oh my, how it rained! Buckets full of water pouring from the sky. Never in my life had I seen rain like this. It was freezing cold and brought refreshing coolness to the sun-scorched city. It also cleansed the dust laden air and rid me of my pesky prickly heat spots, so I welcomed it with open arms.

Farmers also welcomed the seasonal rain. It irrigated the fields of wheat, rice, maize, and cotton. But it came at a risk. Flooding was a common annual occurrence. Farmlands were inevitably inundated, and homes and cattle washed away. City streets would be flooded, too, which was bothersome for the traffic, which even at the best of times was problematic. And in the walled city, with its crude drainage system, the flood water posed a genuine risk to health.

Whilst I still found it difficult to cope without the comforts I had enjoyed in our Home on the Hill – a fridge, washing machine, tumble dryer, cooker, proper toilet, and bathroom with running hot and cold water, not forgetting the car, too, the children seemed to have settled quite happily in their new surroundings.

But children are resilient and do not worry as adults do. They enjoy their meals without thinking where they came from, oblivious of someone else's efforts to prepare them. So long as they are well fed, have fun, and are surrounded by those who love them, children tend to overlook the little inconveniences that impact adults. Even so, I thought they deserved a better place to live, so the desire for a home of our own was often foremost in my prayers.

One of Mustafa's aunts, Ammi Ji's older sister, was a regular visitor. She was a widow, her husband having died suddenly when she was only twenty-five years old, leaving her to bring up her six children alone. I guess she must have been very young when she was married. In those days, it was customary for girls to marry early. Bhai Jan's wife was only thirteen and he was eighteen when they were married, and like most marriages, it was arranged by the parents.

Responsibilities having been thrust upon her at such a young age, Ammi Ji's older sister, *Khala Ji* as we called her, was very astute. She would look at me and instantly know how I was feeling.

"Koi baat nahin, tera saal kai baad kismet badl jati hai, (Don't worry, after thirteen years luck changes)," she said to me one day, which was not much consolation. I was familiar with the superstition that breaking a mirror causes seven years bad luck. But thirteen years! Where did that notion spring from?

So, life went on. And there was a new life to celebrate. It was summer, the worst time of the year to be heavily pregnant. Labour pains started early in the evening, but I didn't tell Mustafa. He was in the sitting room helping his cousin who had a maths exam in the morning. Together, they were going through past papers and solving random questions.

I waited, and waited, wondering if I should disturb them or try to get some sleep. But the way the pains were coming, quicker and stronger, I didn't think the baby would wait that long. Finally, I quietly interrupted and whispered, "Mustafa, I think we need to go to the hospital."

I had no proper ante-natal care. Only home visits by the local midwife, or *daya* as she was called. Expert that she was, she had no kit whatsoever. No sterile gloves, no Pinard stethoscope, and not even a thermometer, but using both hands to feel the foetus she could tell how well the pregnancy was progressing. She even claimed she could tell whether the baby was a boy or a girl. Mine, she was certain was a boy.

Pakistan was, and to a large extent still is, a male dominated society, and the birth of a son invariably merited a celebration. Girls were often unwelcome, and some were even unwanted. There were stories of men divorcing their wives because they had only given birth to daughters, or of taking a second wife hoping she would be the one to provide him with a son; all the result of ignorance, illiteracy and regional customs and traditions, and clearly contrary to the teachings of Islam.

In the time of Prophet Mohammad (may peace and blessings of God be upon him) women were treated like chattel, to be bartered and used at will. Baby girls were generally considered a burden and a disgrace, and many were buried alive. But Mohammad changed all that. He elevated women from the position of slaves to one of respect and dignity and imposed laws to protect them.

He once said to his followers, "The believers who show the most perfect faith are those who have the best morals; and the best of you are those who treat their wives the best."

And in his farewell sermon, a short while before his death, he reminded the men folk of their duty towards women. "You have rights over your wives and your wives have rights over you ... so treat them with kindness," he told them.

Sadly, too many men follow pagan customs, believing them to be Islamic injunctions. They have only to read the Holy Quran and Hadith (sayings and approved actions of the Holy Prophet) to know the true status of women, in both marriage and society, and how men are obliged to behave respectfully and kindly towards them.

Women are the pillars of society. They nurture the new generation. If men abuse, misuse, or subjugate them, you will have a weak nation. But if they honour and respect them and provide them with all the encouragement and appreciation they deserve, you will have a strong nation of confident, well-adjusted people.

Back to me and my labour!

Generally, women in Pakistan were delivered at home, but Mustafa had arranged for me to have the baby in a hospital outside the walled city. It was run by a Christian organisation, and even had a few doctors from England who lived on site. He found a rickshaw and off we went, leaving the children asleep and the cousin busy solving maths problems.

It was a noisy and very bumpy ride, and I felt somewhat guilty, driving crazily fast along the empty road, the cacophonous droning of the rickshaw shattering the silence of the night. There were moments when the rickshaw lurched as it went over a pothole, and several times I hit my head on the bar in front of me, or on the plastic covered roof. I clasped my arms around my precious bulge, hoping the baby would be fine, anxious to reach the hospital in time. Not the best mode of transport for a woman in labour! Or maybe it was! Maybe it shook the baby so much it was in a better position for delivery.

Leaving me in the care of a staff nurse, Mustafa went back home to the children and his student cousin. I had not expected him to leave so soon, but the children needed him more, I told myself. Besides, no one can really do much to help a woman in labour, except the midwives. It is the woman giving birth who has to do all the hard work, and no one else can do it for her.

The nurse who settled me into one of the labour rooms was chatty and cheerful, and quickly made me feel at ease. In fact, she was treating me like a VIP. After excusing herself because she needed to fetch something, she left the room and I could hear her whispering to the other nurses, "A memsahib has come. She's very pretty. And her skin is so white. Go and see!" And two young nurses appeared in the doorway, trying to peep without being seen.

When my nurse returned, she continued chatting, asking me about myself and my family as she went about the routine preparations. And then she asked me which church I attended.

"I don't go to church," I told her. "I'm a Muslim."

Pausing abruptly, and almost reeling backwards, she gasped, "Oh, I thought you must be a Christian."

I explained that I *was* Christian, before I learnt about Islam, at which she looked at me as though I had committed the grossest of crimes.

"How can you abandon Jesus Christ when he died for you on the cross?" she asked, but I did not reply.

I really didn't know what to say, and with contractions coming quicker and ever stronger, I had neither the chance nor energy to answer. She must have been so astonished to discover I was not the Christian she supposed me to be because she left the room and did not return, and another nurse took over.

It *was* a boy! Our second son, born almost exactly one year after the death of Abba Ji. And moments after the birth, the adhan for Fajr prayers began, harmonising with my baby's cries, welcoming him into the world. And then I heard children's voices, English voices, shouting excitedly, "It's raining! It's raining!"

Chacha, who still came every day to collect the tiffin tin for Bhayan, who had taken father's place in the shop, called our new son *Desi Sahib* (local mister) because he was born in Pakistan, and everyone appreciated the name. So, in addition to Bubbles, Jimmy, Beenish, and Biba, we now had Desi Sahib whom we called Desi for short.

Towards the end of the year, things were not looking good for Pakistan. Rumours had it that war with India was imminent. Both nations still bore the scars of partition, and neither was prepared to bury the hatchet. Tensions were rising, and on 3rd December 1971 war broke out. Curfews were imposed and orders were issued for every household to black out all windows to make it difficult for enemy planes to identify their targets at night.

Radio Pakistan relayed news throughout the day as well as patriotic songs. Noor Jehan, Pakistan's Melody Queen, once again rallied the troops as well as the nation with her melodious, soul-stirring renderings of songs like, *Aay Watan Kay Sajeelay Jewan*, *Har Lehza Hai Momin*, and *Eeh Rah-e-Haq ke Shaheedo*; songs made popular during the Indo-Pakistan war of 1965. A war that lasted only seventeen days but caused countless casualties on both sides.

The 1971 war was equally atrocious. It lasted only thirteen days, one of the shortest wars in history, but the worst for Pakistan. As a result, it lost its eastern wing, East Pakistan, which declared independence and became a new country, Bangladesh.

—◆—

All my children had learnt to walk before their first birthday, and Desi Sahib was no exception. At ten months, he was toddling confidently, following his siblings around, babbling away in a language only he understood. And like most toddlers, he was lively and full of mischief.

During the day, Desi would be without a nappy, and generally, I knew when he needed the toilet. At night, however, it was back to wearing a nappy, just to be on the safe side. A towel nappy. No disposable nappies in those days, but thick cotton towel nappies.

Washing them was tricky. A messy, laborious chore that had to be cleverly timed to coincide with an uninterrupted supply of running water. Drying them, however, was not usually a problem. They would dry almost instantly in the summer sun or under the fan. Not like England, where there was often more rain than sunshine in summer, and clothes would freeze on the washing line in winter.

The carpenter who built my kitchen cupboards made a cot for Desi. One morning, I had just finished clearing away after breakfast when I decided to check on Desi who had been asleep in his cot. He was sitting up, chuckling, and clapping his hands, making a smacking sound, both hands covered in what first appeared to be mustard coloured cream, but I could not make out what it was or where he had got it from. And then, to my horror, I realised it had oozed out from the sides of his nappy.

It took me a minute or so to figure out what to do. How to pick him up without getting myself messy? The cot's side could slide down, but the bars were smothered, too, so in the end I lifted him high into the air, out of the cot, and down the stairs to the bathroom, holding him stiffly at arm's length.

I stood him in front of the tub, removed his soiled clothes and prepared to wash him. But, oh my days! The tub was empty. I turned the tap on. No running water, either. Now what?

"Stay there, Desi. Don't move, and don't touch anything."

And I rushed back upstairs to fill a bucket of water from the hamam, which thankfully I had filled earlier that morning. I rushed back down with the heavy bucket, but Desi wasn't where I had left him. He had simply disappeared. I looked around. The front doors were wide open and there, naked, and still messy of course, was Desi, standing on the footrest of a blue Vespa scooter, holding onto the handlebars, and pretending to drive.

"Voom, voom, voom," I could hear him humming.

What to do now? All the women of our house observed purdah. I had rushed downstairs without a dupatta, unaware that the front doors were open, and now the only way to get Desi was to step into the street as I was. There was nothing else I could do, so I grabbed him, rushed back inside, and shut the doors, hoping no one had seen me.

There was no servant at hand whom I could ask to clean the scooter handles. I had no idea who it belonged to or why it was parked immediately outside our house. But one thing was certain. Whoever owned it was in for a stinking shock. May God forgive me! And may the owner of the scooter forgive me, too!

A Nightmare Episode

Autumn 1973. A season that might have ended in tragedy but for a miracle. And another incident involving our little Desi Sahib.

The children were doing what children do best, playing. Weather permitting, they generally played on the roof. There, a wall of about four feet high divided our house from Bhai Jan's. With the help of his siblings, Jimmy had put a broken ladder against it, and while the first one climbed over, he and the others would hold it steady. Turn by turn, they would clamber over the wall. The last one, of course, had no one to steady the ladder so that was always daredevil Jimmy.

One very hot day, shamefully recalled because of the trouble it landed me in, Jimmy led his small troop of minions over the wall and, with the addition of his cousins on the other side, led everyone up the spiral stairs to the topmost roof of Bhai Jan's house where the metal tank that stored all their water was housed, a huge square tank with a round lid that was barely over one foot in diameter.

Jimmy lifted the lid, climbed inside fully clothed, and splashed about, shouting excitedly to the others to join him. But there was only room for one at a time. So, when he had cooled off to his satisfaction, he climbed out and invited the next one in the line to have a dip. It was so high up, and so dangerous, even today the thought of it makes my spine chill.

Of course, the sound of their splashing, clapping, and cheering soon alerted Bhabi Ji who came running to see what all the commotion was about. When she discovered the children were polluting her water supply, she was livid. She then shouted out to me to come quickly and gave me a generous piece of her mind. Her children were not to blame, she claimed. It was Jimmy's idea. He was the one who led them on. She then left me with a warning that I should keep my children under better control.

And that was one of my biggest problems, keeping control. Most of the time I had no idea where the children were or what they were up to. The kitchen door was the main entrance to our home but having to leave it open all hours to allow Ammi Ji access to the hamam had its challenges for me. When I was busy with chores, the children would escape and go off to play with their cousins. But although out of sight, they were never usually far away.

The children were on the roof one afternoon, playing as usual, and after a while Biba came back downstairs for a nap. We usually had tea and biscuits or buttered fruit buns in the afternoon, and whenever I called, the children always came running, but on this particular day, no one answered. No one came.

As there was no response at all, I went upstairs to check on them, but the children were nowhere to be seen. They must be next door, I thought and called over the wall to Bhabi Ji.

"Bachay kahan hai? (Where are the children?)" I asked, expecting her to say they were downstairs playing with her children.

"Mujjay kaya patta? (How do I know?) *Merai do bachay bi ghaib hogai hai* (Two of my children have also disappeared)," was her worried reply.

We called out their names over again, but still no response. Oh my days, I said to myself. What shall I do? Where to begin searching for them? As I ran downstairs to raise the alarm, I suddenly heard their cheerful voices. I looked down to the courtyard below, and there they were, casually entering the front door.

"Where *have* you been?" I yelled.

"Kuku took us to the bazaar to buy some sweets," Jimmy nonchalantly replied, smiling, and clearly at a loss to understand why I was so concerned. Kuku, their eldest cousin, was just as casual.

"Don't ever go out again without asking me," I scolded. "You've no idea how ..."

I paused, and my heart missed a couple of beats as I suddenly realised Desi was not with them. I had watched him carefully make his way up the stairs behind his siblings. And he knew how to come down by himself, sliding backwards over the steps, so I assumed he was with them still. But he wasn't.

"Where's Desi?" I asked. "He was playing with you on the roof. Where is he now? Where did you leave him?" And as I waited for their answer, the nonplussed look on their faces, made my heart race and panic began to take hold of me.

"We don't know," they said. "We left him playing on the roof."

"I've just looked on the roof, but he isn't there. Go and see where he is," I told them, and together they raced upstairs, calling, "Desi! Desi! Where are you?" But there was no reply. Desi was nowhere to be found.

We all gathered in Ammi Ji's room. *"Dua kero, Layla! Dua kero!* (Pray, Layla! Pray!)" she said, and not since Abba Ji's death had I seen her look so worried.

Someone sent for Mustafa. He and his brothers closed the shop and rushed home. And somehow word had spread to nearby relatives that Desi was missing. The enormity and gravity of the situation hit me like a rock when I saw the women silently praying, and Ammi Ji with her *tusbi* (rosary), sliding each bead along as she recited a prayer. Apart from the hushed prayers and clicking of Ammi Ji's beads, the room was eerily silent.

It was clear Desi was nowhere in the house, so everyone presumed he must have followed the children to the bazaar and lost his way. The men were already out in the streets searching. But the bazaar was a crazy, crowded place with little alleys leading to who knows where, and pedestrians jostling alongside bullock carts, loaded donkeys, Vespa scooters, cycles, and push carts. The worst place for a toddler to be, even more hazardous if he was lost and alone.

Only a mother who has lost her child knows how it feels. Most mothers can call on their tremendous reserve of calm and positivity when their child is injured, but when a child is lost it is not knowing where and how the child is, and the feeling of utter helplessness that is paralysing torture. I could sit there no longer.

"*Aao* (Come)!" I said to my daewarani. "Meray saath aao (Come with me)!"

Donning our burkas we went out onto the street to look for little Desi. To say it was like looking for a needle in a haystack is an understatement. And we could not call his name because it was just not done. Women in purdah were neither seen nor heard in public places. It was a mission doomed to fail, but I had to do something.

We stopped at the police station but did not go inside. Instead, we waited outside, hoping someone might find Desi and bring him there. I learned, however, that that was most unlikely. There was a woman standing alongside us and when my daewarani asked her if she had seen a little boy wearing grey shorts and a green T-shirt, she shook her head. Her own ten-year-old son had been missing for six days. There was still no sign of him.

I now understood some Urdu, a lot more than I could speak, and I heard her say that every day children go missing, and that child snatchers often maim them for use as beggars. At that point, my heart jumped into my throat.

"Aou, ghar chaltai hai (Come, let's go home)," I said to my daewarani, my voice barely a whisper.

Almost in a daze now, I rushed back home, my daewarani who had much shorter legs, struggling to keep up with me. The men had been out looking for him. They must have found him by now. He must be home. These were my thoughts as I raced along. And as we passed one street, very close to home, a voice inside told me to look there. But I ignored it.

At home, there was still no Desi, and faces were more solemn than when I had left. All had come to the same conclusion, that there was little hope of finding him. Not today, at least. It was almost time for Maghrib prayers, and it would soon be dark. And while my mind refused to believe he would not be found, my racing, pounding heart was preparing me for the worst. And then I had an idea.

I had often heard announcements from the nearby mosque about someone's death, or *namaz-e-janaza* (funeral prayers before a burial), and even about someone missing.

"Go to the mosque," I told Mustafa, "and ask the Imam to make an announcement over the loudspeaker that our little boy is missing. Tell him what he is wearing and what he looks like. Go, quickly! There is still time before adhan."

"That is exactly what I was thinking," Mustafa replied and set off for the nearby mosque, while we all prayed.

Several minutes passed, but we heard no announcement. Then the call for prayer echoed through the crisp evening air. With no sign of a happy ending in sight, it was my worst nightmare.

The adhan ended. Perhaps Mustafa reached there too late, I thought, and the imam decided to make the announcement afterwards. But that would not be possible, I argued. Immediately after adhan the prayers would begin.

We were sitting, silent and motionless as though ensnared within the gloomiest of clouds. And then suddenly, the front doors flung open.

"I've found him! I've found him!" Mustafa shouted, running across the courtyard, up the stairs, a sleepy and confused Desi in his arms.

"Where was he? Where did you find him?" everyone wanted to know. And Mustafa's answer was so incredible, it was nothing short of a miracle.

He was on his way to the mosque when he met a man carrying what appeared to be just a blanket. They greeted one another, and since they were both walking in the same direction, Mustafa got talking and told him he had lost his little boy and was going to the mosque to ask the Imam to make an announcement, at which the man stopped abruptly. Mustafa stopped, too.

"That's strange," the man said. "I was going to the mosque for the same reason, except I haven't lost a little boy, I've found one." He then lifted the blanket and there was Desi, fast asleep.

The man then explained that the little boy was toddling past his shop and appeared to be alone and very tired, so he picked him up and lay him down on the bench beside him. While Desi slept, he kept an eye on passers-by, expecting someone to come looking for him. But no one came. So, after closing his shop, he decided to take him to the mosque and ask the Imam to make an announcement that a little boy had been found.

Amazingly, the man's shop was along the road the little voice told me to look, the voice I ignored. If it is telling you something good, or guiding you, never ignore that inner voice. Listen and follow it, for it could be your guardian angel.

I shudder to even hazard a guess at what the odds were of finding Desi that day, and what our life would be if we hadn't found him. That this caring, honest man looked after him, and that his and Mustafa's paths crossed on the way to the mosque was truly a miracle. *Alhumdullilah!* (All praise be to God!)

A Telephone Affair

Good news! All this time, Mohammad was not forgotten. He wrote regularly, but the postal service was painfully slow and trunk calls were not only costly but could only be made via the operator and often entailed a long wait. Still, we managed to keep in touch and one day we received the good news that he was coming to Pakistan. Something exciting to look forward to at last!

The children could not wait to see him, and I also counted the days. He was my link to my past and the homeland I had abandoned. Only a person who has experienced it can tell you what home sickness is. The only cure, which in my case was impossible, is to go home.

Mohammad brought presents for everyone. A chunky cable knit jumper for Mustafa, a stylish, pointelle cardigan for me, and a plain but practical cardigan with two generous front pockets for Ammi Ji. Bubbles was over the moon with her gift, a fluffy toy rabbit with long, floppy ears, but would have preferred a real one; and Jimmy was thrilled with his set of dinky cars. A big story book for Beenish, a cute rag doll for Biba, and a clockwork London bus for Desi Sahib!

Mohammad glanced around the room admiringly. The house was new to him. When he left Pakistan, Mustafa was living in a small house in a neighbouring street, the house he used to escort him to in those crazy college days when they were both infected with the romantic movie bug.

"What a great house!" he said to Mustafa. "It's huge! Your father did a marvellous job."

I wanted to interrupt, to tell him that despite its spaciousness, living there was not easy. Running water only twice a day, toilet on the roof, bathroom downstairs, the children free to roam and virtually out of my control, but then I remembered his own postage-stamp house and decided it would be tactless to complain to him of all people. Better to focus on the children and the pleasure of his company, I thought. I also had the sagacity to avoid any topics that might prompt embarrassing questions about how I was managing or how well I could speak Urdu.

All too soon, Mohammad returned to England, and it would be some time before we saw him again.

There was no end to surprises in this new world of mine. A year or so later, Mohammad's mother came to our house to tell us the good news that Mohammad was to be married. She had chosen a girl for him and had arranged the marriage to take place in November when the weather was tolerable. And of course, we were elated that Mohammad would be with us again.

But no! Just as we were planning what we would do and where we would go together, we learnt that he was not coming at all. The marriage would take place in Pakistan with the usual ceremony, but the nikah would be conducted over the telephone. The girl's home was in Rawalpindi, over three hundred miles away. We were all invited, and for the first time, would be travelling by train.

I had already attended Pakistani marriages, so knew what to expect. They were festive, sometimes lavish celebrations, more in line with culture and tradition than religion. Islam promotes simplicity and moderation. It demands that the groom should offer a gift to the bride, whereas in Pakistan and India, and maybe other countries, too, the trend is for the bride's family to provide a dowry commensurate with the family of the groom's expectations.

Undeniably, this imposes untold hardship on the girl's family. It is a malpractice akin to the bartering of women in pagan Arabia, which Prophet Muhammad (may peace and blessings be upon him) put an end to. It saddened and troubled me that people adhere to tradition and social pressure instead of following God's command, and that so many young girls, for want of a dowry, must have felt they were destined for the marriage shelf.

Small wonder that some parents wring their hands and hang their heads in despair when a daughter is born! For no fault of her own she is unwelcome. Baby boys are potential bread winners. Girls are a burden because the fear of dowry overshadows their arrival into the world.

Women are not born to be their husband's slave, as many misguided men believe. Have they not studied the life of the Holy Prophet, Muhammad? How no task was beneath his dignity! How he would mend his own clothes including his shoes, milk the goats, and herd the animals! How well he treated his wives! When given the option of leaving him for a better standard of living, or remaining with him to share his frugal life, they unanimously chose to stay with him. Irrefutable testament to his repute as an ideal husband!

Parents may claim to be Muslim, and yet they choose to follow tradition rather than the teachings of Islam. Many keep the Holy Quran high up on a shelf, but seldom read it, which is like having a treasure trove that is never opened. If you do not open it, how will you know what precious jewels, what pearls of wisdom are stored inside?

—⋅⊰❖⊱⋅—

Back to the marriage!

In those days of small comforts, compared to the lifestyles and amenities of today's world, marriages were a much simpler affair. Generally, no hotel, marriage hall, or special venue, and not even, so far as I can recall, a restroom in sight. And in retrospect, I wonder how we managed.

While some marriages took place in the spacious grounds around or close to the bride's house, in the crowded towns and cities they often took place under a colourful tent specially erected for the ceremony in the street closest to the bride and bridegroom's homes, respectively. Having received invitations well in advance, family and friends would join in the celebrations, an opportunity to meet relatives they might not have seen for ages and enjoy a feast of rich food.

One of my favourites, *gaajar halwa*, was often on the menu as well as kheer, a dessert made from milk, sugar, and rice flour, delicious when mixed with plum chutney, which is how I liked to eat it. On the savoury side, there would be biryani, mutton korma or koftas (spicy meat balls), and saag gosht (spinach with meat). There was sometimes a special addition of roast chicken and fried fish. A feast everyone eagerly awaited and an excuse to overindulge.

Heralded by a blaring, enthusiastic band, the *dulha* (bridegroom), his face obscured by a garland of flowers, would arrive on a bedecked white horse, which for most was the only time they ever experienced a mount. The *dulhan* (bride), traditionally dressed in glittering red, would be nervously awaiting his arrival, her seclusion shared only by close family or friends. Even after the wedding ceremony, she would accompany her husband to his home fully veiled.

A typical Pakistani wedding consisted of three main events – *mehndi, nikah*, and *walima*, which were intrinsically traditional and cultural. The mehndi ceremony was usually a small gathering of close friends and family to celebrate the forthcoming marriage. The bride-to-be, dressed in a yellow ensemble, would have her hands decorated with henna, while others danced and sang to the beat of the *dholak drum*.

The *nikah* or formal marriage ceremony would be performed at the bride's home, conducted by the local *Imam* (leader of the mosque), with recitation of the Holy Quran and prayers for a happy, successful marriage. The groom offers *meher* (monetary amount) to the bride, and the Imam then asks both in turn if they consent to the marriage. Only after saying, *"Qubool hai"* (I accept) three times in the presence of two witnesses, do they sign the marriage contract. And that is when the food is served, much to the relief of all the guests.

The *walima* ceremony takes place at the groom's home, normally the following day. It officially makes the marriage public and is another occasion to enjoy good company and good food.

To anyone unaccustomed to Pakistani marriages, it must seem bizarre that the bride and groom remain apart until the nikah festivities are over. They only see one another face to face, often for the very first time unless they are neighbours or closely related, when they are alone in their bridal room.

In Mohammad's case it was weirder still. There was no cacophonous band accompanying the *barat* (wedding procession). No firecrackers! No garlanded horse! And, strangest of all, no groom! Just a trail of guests, the men in their fancy shalwar suits and matching waistcoats, followed by burka-clad women, their glamourous, glitzy garments well concealed.

On arrival at the dulhan's house, the children and I, along with Mohammad's mother and his sisters, were ushered into the bride's room, while the male guests gathered in the tent outside, all the other women guests occupying a separate, adjoining tent.

The trunk call to Mohammad having been booked well in advance, everyone sat anxiously awaiting the operator's call. Finally, the telephone bell rang, and cries of "Call the Imam!" were urgently relayed from one person to another until he finally appeared and performed the nikah ceremony.

Mohammad's wife would soon be flying alone to England to the husband she had never met; and likewise, Mohammad would be greeting a bride he had never seen.

<hr>

For several weeks after his bride's arrival in England, there was no news from Mohammad. Perhaps he was still settling down to life as a married man after years of bachelorism or enjoying his honeymoon so much that he had forgotten us. We did not know what to think.

His letter finally arrived, but it did not bear good news. He was having serious wife trouble. She was loud and bossy, and at times disrespectful, and he did not know what to do. There was little we could do either, except to write back and encourage him to be patient and pray things would improve. But sometimes, nothing works. Marriage is a risk at the best of times, and one person can never really know another until they live together.

Being an idealist as well as a problem solver, I began to ponder over marriage, why some work out well and others are a complete disaster. Are couples made in heaven? That was my first question. And is there such a thing as the perfect marriage?

It is often said about love, life, or marriage, that it is not a bed of roses but perhaps, I thought, if we identify the thorns and remove them it can become a comfortable one. Part of the problem lies in the fact that our sins and failings are listed on our backs. We can see other's but not our own unless we have the prudence to self-examine.

Undeniably, most marriages are unpredictable and a leap of faith, and so much depends on the part we play. Do we focus on what we want, ignoring our own shortcomings, blaming our spouse when we are also to blame? Do we try to mould them into being what we want them to be, instead of accepting the way they are and appreciating what they have to offer? Is our love conditional, or unconditional? Are we committed or unsure?

Love is so powerful it can move mountains. It can also steer couples in the right direction. A loveless marriage, on the other hand, is a hapless one with little hope from the onset. Their boat might leave the harbour, but turbulent waters almost certainly lie ahead. Some hold on tightly, but often only for the sake of the children.

The most effective instrument in human relationships is love. It has the power to soften the hardest of hearts and mould the most tenacious of minds. And in my Utopian world, two people who love God, and love one another from the purest depths of their heart, exemplify the perfect relationship. Soulmates!

The great British bard, William Shakespeare, beautifully describes love in the following lines of one of his sonnets.

> Let me not to the marriage of true minds
> Admit impediments, love is not love
> Which alters when it alteration finds,
> Or bends with the remover to remove.
> Oh no, it is an ever-fixed mark
> That looks on tempests and is never shaken.

Marriage is generally a more mundane affair. Like two people in a hired boat with no lifejackets and no guarantee from the lender. Some couples may row in unison, gliding peacefully through calm waters, and fighting the turbulent, stormy weather together when it comes, working in harmony to keep the boat steady, focussing on their destination, and keeping passengers safe, too.

Other couples might paddle in different directions, causing the boat to sway perilously. Their focus is on wanting to go their own way, instead of going together. But hey! Look around! You are not the only ones on board. There are passengers, your children perhaps, relying on you to safely navigate the way. Are you going to live up to their expectations and bring them safely back to shore, or are you so selfish that you have no qualms about letting them down, quarrelling, disagreeing, rocking the boat at every meander?

Some couples are so incompatible, they find it impossible to row together, and the only way forward is to abandon ship and go their separate ways. Happiness cannot survive where there is no love and harmony, nor can it be built on another's misery.

Sadly, for some married couples, the boat is doomed to sink. Maybe because there is a gaslighter, spouse-basher on board who thinks the oar, or the fist, is a tool to keep the spouse under control, and the voice an instrument to penetrate the mind to destroy all confidence and self-esteem. The victim needs to abandon ship before things get out of hand and swim to a safer shore.

As for Mustafa and me, we were tolerably compatible, but while he could only see black and white, I could see different shades of grey as well as many colours. And if he had many shortcomings, I am sure I had many more. Despite the differences, we were committed. Our shared faith and the children united us. Besides, I had made promises I could never break, so we kept the boat as steady as we could.

New Horizons

Things were looking brighter for us. Mustafa had come into some money, part of his inheritance. My kerosene stove was replaced by a double burner stove supplied with gas from a bright orange cylinder, the downside being it rested on the floor, so I still had to sit on a low stool to cook. But at least I had two burners, and the frustrating trouble of topping up the noxious kerosene oil and painstakingly rethreading wicks was a thing of the past.

Mustafa also bought a second-hand car. Yes, a car! A grey Mini Morris hatchback, which meant we could go places. One of our favourite places was Tollinton Market. With its wooden verandas and sloping roof, quintessentially colonial in style, it had an exciting ambience about it. And in my mind's eye, I could see the British gentry, men in their military uniforms or fine, tailored suits, and women with their parasols, white gloves, and stylish, full-skirted dresses, strolling past the stalls.

Tollinton Market had so much to offer. There was fresh meat, fish, and vegetables. There were also various food stalls, one of our favourites being the *burger wallah* (burger vendor) where we would have warm, freshly made burgers, our meal for the day. We would then move on to the cakes and bakes to buy biscuits and mouth-watering fruit and coconut macaroons to take home.

But by far our favourite place was the pets' enclosure where puppies, cats and kittens, chickens, rabbits, and several species of birds were for sale. For the children, it was as good as visiting the zoo, although there was an actual zoo close by, and we visited that, too, but not so often. You had to pay to go into the zoo, whereas Tollinton Market was free, although we inevitably ended up spending a lot more on our purchases.

Our next favourite place was Lawrence Park, renamed Bagh-e-Jinnah after Mohammad Ali Jinnah, founder of Pakistan. It had beautiful gardens with gorgeous flowers and different varieties of trees, tall and stately, each bearing a metal inscription of both its botanical and common name.

It also had a small mosque, open canteen, and an imposing Victorian building that housed a huge library of books in English, Urdu, Arabic and Persian. And there were two grand halls where the British used to dance; a building that fascinated me and triggered my imagination. I could visualise the jovial gatherings, the smoking, drinking, singing, feet gliding across the polished floor, long skirts twirling. It gave me a sense of belonging.

The long, wide walkways through the park's garden never failed to liberate my soul, in defiance perhaps of the constraints my burka imposed and the loneliness of my secluded life in the inner city. It meant freedom for the children, too, an exhilarating relief from our treeless, concrete world.

⟡

In Lahore, spring is heralded with a carnival called *Basant*. All day long from early dawn, and even throughout the night, colourful paper kites would fill the sky and shouts of *"Bo kata* (the kite is cut)!" could be heard from the roof tops as one flyer cleverly twirled his thread around that of another's kite and cut it. There was always fierce competition to cut as many kites as possible and collect the spoils to enhance one's collection. And there would be kites of many colours, shapes, and sizes, from the small *sharla* to the giant *patang*.

If Basant was a fun time of the year, it was also a hazardous one. Hospitals would invariably be crammed with kite flyers who had fallen off the roof or been hit by traffic while chasing a drifting kite, the casualty of a *pecha* (kite battle) in the sky. Often, kite strings that had been rolled in powdered glass to make them razor-sharp, or the deadly steel cords some flyers preferred to use, would cut electricity wires, plunging the city into darkness, and leaving live wires dangling dangerously low.

Jimmy was an avid kite enthusiast, and for him and all the children of the inner city, kite-flying began well before Basant and continued afterwards as well, much to my annoyance. To me, it was a dangerous addiction and a total waste of time. But I was an adult. Jimmy was a child.

All sense of time blown away with the breeze and his soaring kite, Jimmy would spend hours on the topmost roof, which gave him the best vantage point. It was virtually impossible to call him down, but when he did come, his eyes red from staring into the sun-filled sky, his fingers cut and bleeding from the cruel string, he would often spend another hour or so repairing damaged kites or making new ones.

Every month of the kite-flying season, I would receive messages from his teacher that he was not paying attention in class and hardly ever did his homework. So, I decided it was time to do something, not only for the sake of his education but for his health and safety. But what? What could I possibly do to kill an obsession that had most of the children of the inner city in its grip?

I tried persuasion, emotional blackmail, scare tactics, even warned him that if he didn't stop wasting all his time flying kites I would destroy them all, but nothing deterred him. And then one day it was raining, and I did the unthinkable. I put all the kites he had collected, all his spoils of kite warfare, outside in the rain. Made from very fine paper, they were ruined instantly. Whether he ever forgave me, I may never know because I was ashamed to ask him, but I hope he did. Thankfully, he gave up kite-flying after that, which is what I intended, and started a new hobby – stamp collecting.

I was not afraid to take tough measures when called for, especially when it meant teaching my children a lesson they needed to learn. I did so once with Bubbles when she was little. She loved peas and always complained that I gave

Jimmy more than I gave her, which was not true. But that is what she thought and how she saw it.

This went on every mealtime, so I decided to put an end to it once and for all. I bought the biggest tin of peas I could find, put one tablespoonful on Jimmy's plate alongside the rest of his food, and put the rest on Bubbles plate. Of course, I knew she could not eat them all, but my ruse worked because she never complained again.

Back to the kites!

The paper from which they were made came in the brightest of colours. Fine and fragile, but at the same time strong. Strong enough to withstand the swirling winds and the slick manoeuvres of the kite flyers. And our local barber, who besides cutting hair did all manner of medical procedures, including circumcision, used it as a tissue adhesive, to mend cuts that would otherwise require stitches.

He would get the patient, and more often than I would like to admit that would be one of my children, to lick a small piece of *guddi gaghaz* (kite paper). He would then stick it onto the cut, holding it firmly in place until it dried and shrank, keeping the skin together. It worked wonders, and left a less visible scar than stitches.

<hr />

The children were now bilingual. They could speak English and Urdu fluently and were also picking up Punjabi words. Ammi Ji was fascinated and thought they were super clever, although it was no extraordinary feat. Children's brains are like sponges. They have the amazing capacity to learn many languages at the same time.

Still, Ammi Ji would repeatedly say, *"Dekho, Layla kay bachay kitnay hushyar hain* (See, how clever Layla's children are). *Woh meray saath Urdu main baat kertay hain, phir apni ammi se angrezi main boltay hain* (they talk to me in Urdu, then speak to their mother in English)."

As for myself, I could understand a lot more than I could speak, although what I knew was not from book learning, which it should have been, but simply from listening to what others were saying. There were words I misheard so inevitably mispronounced, and words for which I completely misunderstood the meanings. And when I did pluck up the courage to speak, all too often I mixed Urdu with Punjabi.

To make things even more difficult for me, sentence construction in Urdu is different. For example, in English I might say, "I am a woman." In Urdu, the same sentence is, *"Mai aik aurat hoon,"* which literally translated is, "I a woman am." The verb does not come immediately after the subject, as in English, and French, but comes at the end of the sentence.

Another problem, which I have yet to overcome, is that in Urdu nouns have genders, which entails matching of noun and verb. *Gaari*, which means car, is feminine, so if I want to say, "the car is going fast," the Urdu for that is, *"gaari taizi se ja rahi hai."*

Many times, instead of saying *"rahi"* (feminine form) at the end of the present continuous form of a verb, I would say, *"raha"* (masculine form), or vice versa, which anyone who heard me found very amusing.

What did it matter, I argued? So far as I was concerned, cars are simply cars. There is no such thing as a female car or male car anyway. But that was the trouble. It did matter. It was one of the rules of conjugation. I should have known better. After all, I studied French in school, and all nouns in French are either masculine or feminine, but it was only the article that had to conform with gender, not verb endings.

It wasn't only gender rules that bothered me. There were some letters of the Urdu alphabet, like the different "t" sounds for example, that I simply could not persuade my tongue to pronounce.

❖

One morning, a memorable one for all the wrong reasons, Ammi Ji was going to visit a sick relative, and as she was leaving she stopped to give me a message for her daughter (my nund). When she returns from college, I should tell her to cook *mutter pilau* (peas with rice) for the evening meal. The peas were already shelled and washed, and the rice was sopping in water, so all my nund had to do was cook it.

"Acha ji, Ammi Ji (Yes, okay, Mother)," I said, as she hurried off down the stairs, her long burka trailing behind her, the sudden rush of air as she descended puffing it up like a parachute.

I must have been too busy with the children to notice my nund arrive home from college, but it was early still, and Ammi Ji was not due back till evening, so I waited an hour or so and then went to give her the message.

I found her reclined in an armchair, listening to Abba Ji's old radio, her feet resting on the table. It was tuned to an Indian programme of songs by popular playback singers. Lata Mangeshkar, Asha Bhosle, Mohammad Rafi, Kishore Kumar, and others. I loved Indian and Pakistani songs; and of all the singers in the world, none can surpass the nightingales, both male and female, of the Indian sub-continent. The deep sentiments of the lyrics and mellow melodies accompanied by the sitar, an instrument that pulls at the heart strings!

Mohammad Rafi's mellifluous rendering of one of his signature songs, *"Kya Hua Tera Wada"* (What has become of your promise?) was playing, enchanting listeners around the world, while my nund, eyes tightly shut, seemed to be lost in her own Utopia. I called her name several times, but she did not respond. She was fast sleep. So, I decided to leave her and come back later, which was a big mistake.

Ammi Ji arrived back home much earlier than expected and the first person she met at the top of the stairs was me. She asked me if I had passed on her message and I nonchalantly and honestly replied, *"Naheen, Ammi Ji* (No, Ammi Ji)", at which she eyed me quizzically and asked, *"Kiyoun* (why)?"

"*Woh so raha hai* (She's sleeping)," was my nonchalant reply. And then I added, by way of explanation, "*Woh haramzadi hai.*"

Ammi Ji stared at me, her eyes as wide as saucers, her brain clearly struggling to digest what I had said. "*Kiya kaha tumnay* (What did you say)?" she asked.

And like a simpleton, I repeated what I had just said. "*Woh so raha hai. Woh haramzadi hai.*"

She seemed genuinely shocked, and I could not understand what I had said to upset her, and to make matters worse Mustafa arrived on the scene. He was home early, too. "What did you say to Ammi Ji?" he asked, and I repeated it for a third time.

Mustafa slapped his hands on his forehead. "Where did you learn that?" he gasped. "Do you even know what it means?"

"Yes! It means someone who takes it easy like a princess," I calmly replied, confident that he and Ammi Ji would now let me off the hook. But it was not yet over.

Mustafa made me apologise to Ammi Ji and then dragged me into the sitting room. Apparently, I had done the unthinkable. Again! And this time I had insulted my mother-in-law as well as my nund.

"Don't ever use that word again," he warned me. "It's a swear word. And it might help if you don't try to speak Urdu without me."

I did not want to argue and prolong the unpleasantness, but I still could not understand what I had said wrong, and although I insisted, Mustafa would not tell me what his version of *"haramzadi"* was.

"You don't need to know," he said. "Just make sure you never say it again."

Up to that point, I had been proud of my linguistic progress. I had managed to pick up many words, simply by listening, and I was usually pretty good at guessing the meanings. I must have heard someone saying *haramzadi*, and as far as I understood, it simply meant *"aaram kernay waali shehzadi"* (a princess who takes it easy); *haraam* or *aaram* meaning "taking it easy", and *zadi* being short for *"shehzadi"* (princess). So I couldn't understand what all the fuss about. Imagine my embarrassment when I learnt it meant bastard!

Tsunami

One of Ammi Ji's regular visitors was *Khala Ji* who lived close by. Before leaving, she would always pop in to say *salaam* to me and ask me how I was. That she seemed genuinely concerned was like a tonic. It lifted my spirits and I thanked her for it. But Khala Ji was old, and her health was fast failing. And then came the day when Ammi Ji received news that she was so unwell her family had gathered around her to pray. Leaving the children with Mustafa, I donned my burka and accompanied our women folk to Khala Ji's home.

When we arrived, she was conscious but unable to speak and her breathing was very laboured. Everyone knew she was dying and began to pray that God would take her soul gently and grant her a place in Paradise. About an hour later, she took her last breath, and we stayed on to pray.

Her death deeply affected me. She had been a constant well-wisher and silent friend. She knew me, without really getting to know me, a quality only people with pure hearts possess.

Prayer always rekindled my spirit. Personal prayers can be said any time and any place, and I cherished those moments of quiet meditation. I also loved the formal Muslims prayers, an exercise of discipline, obedience, and submission to our Creator.

For the children, it was often a fun time. A little one would ride on my back as I bent down or sit on my knee when I was in the sitting position. And sometimes, I would have two little ones praying with me, one on each knee, and another on my back.

In no other religion is there a discipline like Islamic formal prayer, and scientist have yet to discover the comprehensiveness of its physiological benefits. While the act of obedience, submission, and worship is spiritually uplifting, each body movement is also physically beneficial. The entire body is gently exercised, even internal organs. I know for sure, that any aches and pains I had, particularly backache, would often be gently eased away as I said my prayers.

Once, the Holy Prophet Muhammad (May peace and blessings of Allah be upon him) was going to the mosque to lead the prayer when he passed by a man lying curled up on his bed. When the Prophet asked him why he was lying there, the man told him he had stomach-ache, at which the prophet advised him to come to the mosque to pray. "You will feel better afterwards," he told him.

I like it that in the Quran, whenever God commands us to do something, He often follows with the words, "That is better for you." He made us, so He knows precisely what we need, what we should do to make the best of life, what benefits us individually and as a society.

When we do *wudhu*, the ablution before prayer, we wash specific parts three times each, beginning with our hands, then mouth, inside our nose, full face, and our arms up to the elbows from wrist downwards. All acts of obedience, but also good hygiene to avoid catching and spreading diseases. Passing wet hands over our head and back of the neck, cleaning inside and behind the ears, washing our feet, taking care to clean in between each toe. These are not intended as a ritual only but to cleanse the body and help prevent diseases.

As time went by, I began to embrace life in Lahore. The cultural and historical heart of Pakistan, Lahore was a mesmerising marriage of its illustrious past and British colonial rule. And while the identity of the walled city was still alien to me and quintessentially Indian, outside it the vestiges of British presence instilled a feeling of belonging. I was not alone. Many before me had walked these streets and called this city home.

The buildings, the names of places and streets, evoked a sense of home from home. Lawrence Road, named after John Lawrence, Viceroy of India. Tollinton market, which was originally built to house an exhibition of Punjab arts and industries, but later turned into a market and named after H. P. Tollinton, Financial Commissioner and Secretary, Punjab Government. And places like St Anthony's Cathedral, Mall Road, Lower Mall, Hall Road, Mason Road, Jail Road, Lytton Road, and many more, rang a bell of familiarity.

Thanks to our Mini Morris, I could go shopping on Mall Road and browse in my favourite shops, Ferozsons Book Shop, Bata shoes, and the departmental store, H. Karim Buksh where I bought most of the children's clothes, especially at sale time. I was also becoming familiar with Lahore's cultural, historical landmarks.

Standing proudly in the centre of the road outside Lahore Museum is a massive canon named Kim's Gun, cast during the reign of Ahmad Shah Durrani, another testament to Lahore's powerful past. An even more imposing icon is the magnificent Badshahi Mosque, a classic example of Mughal architect, built during the reign of Emperor Aurangzeb when Lahore was the Mughal capital of India.

Close by, stands the Lahore Fort, which dates to emperors Akbar, Shah Jahan, and Aurangzeb, and famous for its *Sheesh Mahal*, Palace of Mirrors, commissioned by Shah Jahan to reflect the spectacle of classical dancing he so relished. Adorned in dazzling, full-skirted dresses, tantalizing veils, and *ghunghru* (bells) around their ankles, the dancers would perform exclusively for the emperor's pleasure.

And there was the Wazir Khan Mosque, built during the reign of Shah Jahan. Exquisitely embellished with intricate Persian-style tile work, and elaborate frescoes depicting the Mughal Era, it is considered Lahore's most ornately decorated mosque.

In the days of the Mughal emperors, the city of Lahore was surrounded by a brick wall about nine metres high, interrupted by thirteen gates: Delhi Gate, Roshnai Gate,

Akbari Gate, Yakki Gate, Bhati Gate, Sheranwala Gate (also once known as Khizri Gate), Lohari or Lahori Gate, Kashmiri Gate, Mori Gate, Masti Gate, Shah Alami Gate (once known as Bherwala Darwaza), Taxali Gate (once called Lakhi Gate), and Mochi Gate.

Most having been destroyed, only six gates remain, but they are bereft of their original opulence, and for some only the archways remain. A solemn reminder of the city's splendiferous past.

A day trip took us once to *Shalimar Bagh* (Shalimar Gardens). A magnificent, romantic place if ever there was one. Built by the Mughal royals as a private paradise where they could relax and entertain friends, its elaborate water features represent the harmony between man and nature, and heaven and earth.

On my mental calendar, I marked each year, eager for the thirteen years to pass, hopeful of brighter days ahead when I would have a home of my own, with garden and trees and space for the children to play. But time is capricious. When you wish it would fly by, it goes painfully slowly. And sometimes, it comes and is gone before you know it. In between, however, wonderful things can and do happen.

The beginning of 1978!

The birth of our third son, and the heavyweight of our small clan, weighing in at eight and a half pounds. I remember struggling in the final stage of labour when one of the nurses was urging me to push.

"I can't," I said, breathing heavily. "It feels like a sack of potatoes." At which the other nurses in the room giggled.

"It's not a sack of potatoes," she insisted. "It's a baby, So, push! With the next pain, push as long and as hard as you can."

I tried with the next contraction, but the baby still did not budge. And in Urdu I said to her, *"Isaay ander hi rehnay do* (let it stay inside)."

And while the other nurses chuckled again, my nurse remained stern and firm. "No!" she said. "That's just not possible. You will have to push harder. Now!"

For several days, we did not name him. Deciding on a proper name always took serious deliberation, whereas pet names were more of a pronto affair. Bhai Jan wanted to call him *Gongloo* (swede) because he had big, round cheeks. And an uncle, amused by the baby's double chin, called him Winston Churchill. In the end, we called him Tommy.

Now more than ever, with a family of six children, I felt the need for our own home, but a need, a desire, that was almost exclusively mine. Bhai Jan had recently sold his house next door and moved to a spacious bungalow in a beautiful part of the outer city. Bubbles' dream of owning a pony, or even a donkey, had long since faded. All she asked for now was a pet rabbit, but where to keep one in our House of Doors?

An occasional *tonga* ride was some consolation, though. If we were going somewhere where the roads were too problematic for our little Mini, Mustafa would hire a tonga. He and Bubbles would sit in the front, next to the *tonga wallah* (tonga driver). Somewhat risky but exhilarating! And we would all sit behind, a balancing act if ever there was one, and just as dangerous as sitting up front.

Inside the walled city, traffic was invariably chaotic, and whenever the tonga wallah had to pull on the reins, forcing an emergency stop, the tonga would lurch backwards, then forwards, and both front and back passengers were in danger of being thrust onto the road, something that rarely happened but could, so holding on tightly was crucial.

It had been ages since we had seen Mohammad, but one day a letter arrived saying he was coming for a short visit to Pakistan with his wife and two little boys. Once the carefree bachelor, uncle, and friend, he was now a family man with children of his own.

Mohammad was never deemed a handsome man. A winsome smile? Yes, undeniably so! Charming, sociable, generous, and good-hearted? Definitely! But not handsome. His wife, on the other hand, though a little overweight since the birth of her children, was very beautiful, and the boys resembled her. With their plump, rosy cheeks and long, curly hair, they reminded me of Raphael's *Cherubs from the Sistine Madonna*.

They had not been in Lahore long when his mother's health suddenly took a turn for the worse. Besides her enduring illness, she was getting on in years, so Mustafa and I went to see her.

She was lying on her charpai, noticeably pale and weak. She turned her head and looked directly at me with unusually dull eyes. She then put her hands together and whispered, *"Mujhay maaf kerna* (forgive me),"* which puzzled me. She had never wished me any harm, so why was she asking me to forgive her? Later, I learnt that when people knew they were dying, they would ask God to forgive them, as well as the people around them, in case they had unknowingly wronged or offended them.

We had barely reached home when Mohammad came to tell us she had died. Another shock, another family member gone. But that is life! A perpetual juxtaposition of sadness and joy, birth, and death.

Life went on! But like unrequited love, unfulfilled desires weigh heavily upon one's shoulders. A move to a place of our own in pastures green was not on the horizon, and I felt buried under the rubble of my shattered dreams. I should have been more optimistic, I know. I should have seen that the glass was half full, not half empty, but I didn't. Despair had managed to get a firm hold on me.

Mankind is born weak, and I am no exception. Often, we create our own misery instead of looking for happiness. That is a human failing. As is weakness of faith. Even knowing that God is in control and has the power to hear and answer our prayers, to change our fortunes, still we harbour doubts and allow despair to supplant hope, undermining our faith in the process. *Melancholy* reflects my feelings at that time when my spirits were low.

Melancholy

Uninvited, Melancholy creeps into our lives. It descends upon us in those trying days of our youth when we are lagging, when we fail to identify with our peers, or when we find ourselves outside life's mainstream, feeling lost and alone.

Melancholy's sombre words penetrate our fragile, troubled minds, and its hands weigh heavily upon us, forcing a flow of tears to wash away our inhibitions, hopelessness, anxieties, and fears. And that is when we pick ourselves up and re-join the clan to which we belong.

Having found our place in the boat destined to carry us through life, we sail on; and the wind, at times sweet-scented, calm, and refreshing, but oftentimes forceful, fierce, and stressful, moves us ever onwards to our destination.

And then that perplexing time when Melancholy descends upon us more frequently. We recognise it well, the fleeting visitor that called to warn, awaken, and urge us to belong. But unlike the transitory visitor of our youth, it lingers, and brings a new, more urgent message. A new tenderness in its voice, it whispers, "Yes, you belonged. And still you belong, but not here."

It then points beyond to a signpost and a sea of small boats, bobbing harmoniously to the rhythm of the waves. "There is where you now belong. That is your destination."

"Welcome!" says the sign; and beyond it the sea sparkles with a brilliance never seen before, its waters surging towards the heavens. Complacently, Melancholy smiles, knowing that having seen what lies ahead, we have understood. But to be sure, it speaks again.

"You have sailed well in all kinds of weather, but now it is time to leave the big boats behind. They have young hands to steer them, new seas to cross, new lands of treasure, hopes and dreams to discover. Time now, to take account of all you have achieved, all the things you have touched and changed forever, all your failings and regrets. Time now, to board one of the little boats and sail alone across the Ocean of Eternity."

After writing Melancholy, I realised the need for some serious soul-searching. I said my prayers regularly, five times a day, even Tahajud most nights. But obedience and prayer do not denote piety or faith. So, how strong was my faith, I wanted to know? Rather, how weak was it, and why?

Faith is not believing in God when things are going your way, nor is it believing when you see incredible things happening before your very eyes. Faith is to believe when the going is tough, when you cannot see the light at the end of the tunnel, and yet you know, as sure as there is day and night, that it is there.

<hr />

In late summer of the same year, we were struck by a tsunami of grief that shattered the foundations of our family.

Following his move to the outer city, Bhai Jan frequently came to see Ammi Ji. After all, he had spent his entire life living with her, his father too until his death, so it was only natural for him to visit. But then he started coming every day, and I began to suspect something might be preying on his mind.

One day, we were all sitting in Ammi Ji's room when Bhai Jan arrived. Sitting down on the charpai beside her, he said, "Ammi Ji, today I walked along all the streets where I used to play, and I passed by our old house, too." And he named several other places that held boyhood memories.

He seemed elated, and I remember watching him intently, trying to fathom why he seemed so interested in his past.

Why was he wandering down those memory lanes as though paying homage to old places and times gone by?

A few days later, we received the devastating news that Bhai Jan had suffered a massive heart attack and had been rushed to hospital. Mustafa was with him when he suffered another, fatal attack a couple of hours later. Bhai Jan was no more.

Abba Ji's death had left us numb, and it had taken time for wounds to heal. We all knew he had an ailing heart and was getting on in years. Even then, nothing prepares you for death, and in many ways it was more difficult to come to terms with Bhai Jan's sudden passing away. He was only in his mid-forties and had always been so full of life.

The following months were difficult for me. My children, as always, were my life. They would do and say funny things, transforming a sombre ambience into one of joy and positivity. They were my all and everything. But they were also my responsibility and I felt I was failing them. When Bhai Jan lived next door, his friendly, smiling appearance early every morning and joyful greeting was a cheerful start to my day. Like Abba Ji, he had shown me kindness. A silent admirer, and undeclared friend.

A dark cloud loomed above me after Bhai Jan's death, and I struggled to see the sunshine. Living in my House of Doors, at times ostracized through petty quarrels that should never had happened, I longed for a friend to share my thoughts and feelings, aspirations, and despair. Death comes to each one of us, sooner or later, I thought, so maybe what happens in between doesn't really matter, hence my poem, Surrender.

Surrender

My mind drifted freely twixt heaven and
earth.
No need, thought I, of footprints in the
sand.
Light-winged as the clouds, fly high
And let the streams of life flow by.
Hold not the past for it has been and fled.
The future, uncertain and unseen, is out
of reach,
And the present is too painful to embrace.
So, fly on! Forget all strife.
Feel not the drag, the weariness of life,
For life is but a borrowed gift, and the
Lender waits.
Borrowed time, borrowed breath, borrowed
body, mind and soul,
Obediently awaiting His call.
A call as inevitable as all things are
ephemeral.
And so, I drift along; desires all dissipating
with the breeze,
All grief laid to rest. And I surrender.
For what was never mine, nor ever will be,
cannot be mine today.
All but my heart surrender. Only my heart
complains.
Is it too borrowed? Or is it mine?
And will the feelings therein remain?

A Troublemaker

It was about this time that I had a recurring dream. I would be walking along an unfamiliar path, aware that someone was following me, but when I stopped to look behind, there was no one. And then, one night, in my dream, I was walking along the same path, but this time when I stopped and turned round, I came face to face with someone tall and fair with a pleasing presence. Someone I had never seen before.

"Why are you following me?" I asked, to which he or she (I could not tell) replied, "I am following to make sure you are alright."

After that, the dreams ended. But it left me with the feeling that I was not alone. Someone was watching over me. Was it an angel? Was it someone who was about to cross my path? Or just my own imagination translating into a dream? I did not know. Even so, it comforted me.

Suddenly, my world became interesting. I was still without any social life beyond the doors and walls of my inner-city home, something I craved. I longed for a friend who could understand me and had perhaps made a similar cultural transition and journey. But there was no teahouse or coffee culture in those days, not that I was aware of or had the freedom to explore, and Mustafa had no such acquaintances. So, the chances of meeting and making friends was very slim indeed.

But we now had a television, which in many ways made up for the lack of any social life. A welcome consolation that kept me occupied and entertained. I could watch the daily news, Urdu dramas, even English films. Mostly American, actually.

We enjoyed more family time, sitting together and watching a bonanza of programmes. One of them was, in fact, called *Bonanza*. There was a wide selection of children's programmes. *The Six Million Dollar Man*, *The Bionic Woman*, *Chips*, *Little House on the Prairie*, *Skippy*, which I also loved to watch; *The Lucy Show*, and *Mind Your Language*, two of my favourites.

There were countless adult Urdu dramas, riveting and atmospheric, and void of indecencies so the children could also watch. Popular comedy series, *Alif Noon*, and *Sona Chandi* never failed to entertain us, while serious dramas like *Andhera Ujala*, *Ankahi*, *Dhoop Kinare*, and *Waris* were very addictive. With so much to watch and enjoy, we were spoilt for choice; and luckily, only one channel, so no quarrels over which programme to watch.

We also acquired a refrigerator. Small, but convenient all the same. No more sour milk or yogurt, and bottles of cold water during the long, thirsty, summer days and nights. And one of the first things I did was make a trifle, sweet memory of times gone by.

Bubbles was now in college, aspiring to become a doctor, with Beenish following in her footsteps. Jimmy wanted to go to England and become a cricketer. Academics, he had decided, were not for him. In many ways, he was so like his uncle, Bhai Jan, who had been a very reluctant student and barely passed eighth grade. His teachers had given up on him, and since his parents could not persuade him to take study seriously, he ended up working alongside his father, helping to run the family business. And in that he excelled.

There was one teacher who was exasperated by Bhai Jan's flippant attitude. He taught geography, and when he asked the class, "Why is the earth round?" Bhai Jan shot his hand up and replied, "Because your glasses are round, Sir," at which the whole class burst into laughter.

Similarly, when Jimmy had to write an essay on a cricket match, he wrote just one line – Rain stopped play! On another occasion, when the topic of the essay was My Favourite Teacher, he crossed out the "cher" and wrote, My favourite tea is Brooke Bond.

Unfairly regarded as her brother's keeper, poor Bubbles was frequently called into the office by his class teacher who would show her what Jimmy had written. I also received regular complaints from different subject teachers, asking, pleading, "What shall we do with him?" But none of us could find the answer. Polite persuasion, encouragement, reward, reasoning, punishment, threats – nothing worked. Jimmy was incorrigible. Our only hope was that over time he would reform himself. And eventually, he did.

Biba and Desi seemed to have no ambitions and were simply enjoying school and life in general. Tommy was still too young to go. And then there was one more late addition to our clan, our fourth daughter. We were now a family of nine – Mustafa, me, and seven children, *Masha'Allah!* What God has willed!

It was little Tommy who found just the right pet name for our new baby girl. Before her birth, we watched an Indian film called *Noori*. In the film was a song, *Noori*, which Tommy loved, and he could be heard singing to himself, "Noori, Noori," as he played. And when he came to see me in the hospital, he asked, "Where is Noori?" So that is what we called her.

Unlike today's fast-paced world, I enjoyed the privilege of being just a mother and housewife. That was a time when women in Pakistan did not generally go to work, men traditionally being the breadwinners. But for any society to function well, women have a role to play in the workforce. Without women, hospitals, schools, and colleges, to name a few, would close. And professional women usually managed to balance work, children, and family life very well, especially if they had the support of a joint family setup.

As a housewife, I had time to enjoy many precious moments with my children. Little Noori being the last, and the other children off to school, I had more time to enjoy those fleeting days of her babyhood. I would often sit her on my lap and kiss her soft forehead over and over, singing, *"Meri jaan,"* (My life) a term of endearment.

One day, Mustafa's elder sister saw me and commented, "You love her so much as though you could never part with her, but she'll grow up and then you will have to find a husband for her. But how will you let her go?"

"I won't," I replied. "But if I do, I'll only marry her to a prince."

By the end of each day, I was usually worn out and looking forward to Mustafa's return from the market. The children were, too. Even when the television was on, we could hear him striding across the courtyard and up the stairs, and one of the children would announce, "Daddy's here!" But then the sound of his footsteps could be heard going past our doors, heading for Ammi Ji's room, which is where the two brothers and younger sister would gather in the evening.

Bhayan had the wisdom to meet and greet his family first, have the meal his wife had prepared for him, and then make his way to Ammi Ji's. But not Mustafa. He would go directly to his mother's room to listen to the family's current affairs, in other words, gossip. And frequently on the agenda would be something I or the children had said or done.

Bubbles had not said "salaam" to a visiting aunt, Jimmy had been up to some mischief again. Whatever it was, it was always my fault. But worse, far worse, was when I had said something out of place or quarrelled with someone. Like the time I was on the blacklist for calling my daewarani the worst English swear word imaginable. It happened like this.

Her son hit Biba on the head with the heavy end of a jharu, which hurt and made her cry. I picked her up to comfort her and was not going to say anything. Children are always fighting and making up again, so I usually had the prudence not to interfere but leave them to sort it out. However, my daewarani came on the scene, and without knowing what had happened, commented, *"Woh humeesha roti rehti hay* (She's always crying)," meaning Biba, which was not true. In fact, it was far from the truth. Biba was a very happy child, always smiling and laughing at the smallest pleasure.

When I replied that Biba was crying because her son had just hit her on the head, she denied it outright, at which I said, as best as I could in Urdu, that since she was not even there and had not seen what happened, how could she say with such certainty that her son did not hit Biba? I was there, and I saw it.

Escalating the situation from the sublime to the ridiculous, she then called her servant girl who had been completely out of sight cleaning the middle room, and asked her, *"Kiya usnay usko maara tha* (Did he beat her?)?"

The poor girl did not know what to say. She had no idea what was going on, but my daewarani was prompting her to reply and deny. And that is when, utterly incensed by her ludicrous behaviour, I shouted, "You stupid woman!"

With a shocked expression, eyes flickering as if she were about to faint, she went running to tell Ammi Ji that I had just hurled what she claimed was the obscenest English abuse at her. And, unable to explain that the word stupid was not a swear word and that I had used it merely to reprimand her, I was branded *budtameez* (rude) and a troublemaker, a reputation I repeatedly battled to amend thereafter.

Mishaps Galore

Our Mini Morris might have been a small car, but she had a very big heart. Hmmm! I cannot believe I just wrote that. I would get annoyed and thought it ridiculous that in Urdu innate objects have genders. But I take it back. Our Mini was one of the family. She took us everywhere we needed or wanted to go. It was not her fault that we took short cuts and ended up lost or ran out of petrol miles from the nearest petrol station.

She (it must be *she* because *gaari* is feminine, remember) took the children to school or college every day. She took them to their friends' homes, to parties and school and college events. And it was a wonder how we all managed to fit in, but we did.

One day, we were cruising along the canal, windows open, breathing in the fresh air and admiring the trees on either side, when we became aware of a strange smell, like something electrical burning. And then I noticed smoke drifting upwards from between my feet.

"The car's burning!" I shouted to Mustafa, panic in my voice.

Mustafa braked suddenly, jumped out, and opened all the doors. Smoke was now billowing from beneath the back seat that housed the battery. And while some passers-by rushed to the rescue, others looked on in astonishment as, one by one, we all got out of the car. Six children, and a burka clad woman with a baby in her arms! They could not believe their eyes.

Mini was pushed to the workshop by Mustafa and several willing helpers while we sat on the grassy banks of the canal, anxiously awaiting her safe return. It seemed to take forever, but we had pleasant, green surroundings for a change and could sit under the shade of the trees, always a welcome treat. Sighs of relief mingled with shouts of joy when our faithful Mini finally came chugging back.

One long school vacation, which coincided with the worst season of the year, the Monsoon, we had promised to take the children to the cinema on Regal Chowk to see *The Crazy Boys of the Games*, a French comedy film with English sub-titles. Although it had rained heavily and relentlessly all morning, there was a welcome break in the weather, so we ventured out.

Our street was flooded, over a foot deep, which should have made us think twice about going anywhere, let alone the other side of the city. But no! We all clambered into the car and off we went.

Midway between home and the cinema the flood waters deepened, and we spotted several vehicles that had obviously stalled. From all directions, youths were dashing around like super-heroes, splashing through the water to rescue them. Ignoring our Mini's coughing and spluttering, we ploughed on, our feet held high to avoid the rising water that was now almost level with the seats. And then, still coughing and choking, warning us that she was drowning, poor Mini stalled.

Several lads came rushing to our aid. "Don't worry, we'll get you going again," one of them shouted, and they pushed our little Mini till she was on higher, dryer ground.

"Now you can get home safely," one of the lad's said, pleased that he had helped another victim of the Monsoon rains. We thanked him and his friends, not daring to tell them we were bound for the cinema, not home.

Over the years, we had our fair share of accidents and illnesses. Measles, mumps, scarlet fever, coughs, colds, earache, and upset tummies! Cuts, grazes, and bruises! A broken arm – that was Bubbles who fell on the stairs, helped by Jimmy (she said he pushed her).

Jaundice! That was me, just before the war with India. I was feeling very groggy, and when I happened to glance in the mirror, I noticed the whites of my eyes were the colour of egg yolks. My skin was yellowed, too. Avoid all fats! That's what the doctor ordered. Ammi Ji, however, insisted on calling her trusted friend, *Bibi Behn* to cure me, *desi style*.

Bibi Behn arrived with a small twig, small clay dish, small bottle of mustard oil, and a small packet of turmeric. She tipped all the turmeric powder into the dish, poured a measured amount of mustard oil onto it, and then mixed vigorously with the twig, all the while her lips moving rapidly as if reciting a prayer.

Although somewhat accustomed to all kinds of bizarre happenings, I still harboured doubts, and as I looked on, wondering what she was going to do with this dark yellow concoction, my heart began to race over a hundred beats a minute. Was she going to massage me with it? Ask me to swallow it? Luckily, it was neither.

When she was satisfied it was well-blended, she held the pot high, circled it three times over my head, and then tipped the contents down the drain. Done! I was cured. Well, not quite. Bibi Behn, who could neither speak nor understand English smiled at me and held up three fingers. *"Teen dafa karna* (Must do it three times). *Mein kal aur persun ayungi* (I shall come tomorrow and the day after)."*

Of course, I had no doubt that it was a sheer fallacy, but Bibi Behn, bless her, believed it to be a cure, Ammi Ji too, and it was their sincere intention to cure me.

The following day, Mustafa was fixing blackout paper to the roshandans. He was at the top of a very long ladder, and I was holding onto it to stop it from slipping. But then Ammi Ji called me with an urgency in her voice, so I left the ladder and went to the doorway to answer her. Bibi Behn had arrived and was waiting to dispense the second potion to cure my jaundice.

I called out to Ammi Ji to say that I was coming and then looked back at Mustafa. The ladder was slowly sliding downwards with him clinging desperately onto it. He should have jumped off, but he didn't. He clung on as if he thought the ladder would save him. And then, suddenly gaining momentum, the ladder came crashing down.

I rushed to help him onto his feet. He looked awful. One eye was completely bloodshot, and he was shaking with shock. He did not complain about his finger, that it was hurting or looked distorted, and none of us noticed, we were all so concerned about his eye and possible damage to his vision.

Over a week passed, his eye slowly improved, and we thanked Allah that his eyesight had been saved. Only then did he show us the broken finger. But because it did not cause him any pain, Mustafa decided to do nothing about it. So, it healed the way it was. Bent downwards by several degrees!

Tommy did not escape injury. Like his older brother, he had a craze for kite flying. He had been tracing the progress of a drifting kite and watched it land on the roof of the mosque, at least six feet below ours. He jumped down to retrieve it, landing with a painful thud and a twisted ankle that instantly swelled like a balloon. He was in a lot of pain, so Mustafa rushed him to the nearby *pehlwaan* (wrestler) who knew all about muscle and ligament traumas. He came back home with a heavily bandaged foot, reeking of the pehlwaan's special ointment. But in time, it healed well.

⊰⊱

Incredibly, just a couple of weeks after Desi's scary misadventure in the bazaar, being lost and then miraculously found, he had an accident on the stairs that scarred him for life.

Desi Sahib had been on the roof, playing with the other children, when he decided to come back downstairs, but instead of coming down our stairs, he chose to come down the stairs on the opposite side, where Bhayan's rooms were, and it was not uncommon for my daewarani to use the stairs on her side for cooking.

She would put her kerosene stove on the second step, but before lighting it to start cooking, she would close the door at the top of the stairs to prevent anyone from entering. On that fateful day, however, she forgot to close it. So, as little Desi made his way down her stairs, he was completely unaware that he was sliding into danger.

There were about fifteen steps, and because of the bend in the stairway, she was equally unaware that Desi was descending. An adult or older child coming down the normal way would see the stove, go back up and use the other stairs. But Desi was a toddler, and he was coming down backwards.

Having made the saalan, or curry, in a copper pan, she put the loose-fitting lid on it and placed it on the third step. She then put the tuwa (griddle) on the stove to heat up and went inside to get the bowl of chapati dough. It was then that Desi went crashing into everything. His foot slid on the loose lid of the pan, toppling it, and spilling the hot curry, and like a domino effect, the pan knocked over the tawa and the oil stove.

The sound of the mighty banging and clanging sent everyone rushing to see what had happened. Luckily, Bhayan was home, and swiftly lifted Desi from the flames. Though noticeably shocked, little Desi did not cry.

"What's that?" I asked, pointing to what looked like onion peelings on one of Desi's legs.

Bhayan quickly turned Desi towards him so I could not see. *"Mat dekho!* (Don't look!)" he said, but I had seen enough to realise it was not onion peelings at all, but Desi's burned and blackened skin.

Every day, I had to change the special burn dressings, and my stomach would churn at the sight of his raw, oozing skin. But not once did little Desi cry.

Bubbles survived measles and scarlet fever, as well as an electric shock, which was no surprise. The electrics were hazardous in the best of homes since there were generally no earth or circuit breakers. Pylons would become live during heavy rain, and we would often hear of cattle bumping their bulging bellies against one and being electrocuted. Sometimes, it was people.

Beenish once had typhoid but was quickly diagnosed by Mustafa's doctor cousin who came to our home to examine her. With the appropriate treatment of Chloramphenicol tablets she quickly recovered.

Several months later, when Biba became ill with a fever, the cousin was out of city, so we took her to a child specialist, supposedly the best in Lahore. No blood test, just a temperature check and a feel of her tummy and his diagnosis was the weirdest I had ever heard.

She had a latent amoeba in her intestines that had now become active, he told us, and prescribed so many different medicines, I wondered how we would ever be able to administer them to a child who had completely lost her appetite as well as half her body weight.

After two days, it was obvious the medicines were not helping. In fact, she was getting worse. So we decided to take her to another doctor, also a child specialist. I remember carrying her effortlessly down the stairs, she was so light.

To my utter surprise and disappointment, the doctor seemed clueless. He suspected pneumonia, but I was not convinced. Even with my layman's eyes, I could see no such signs. The problem was not with her lungs but her intestines.

"Do you think she might have typhoid?" I suggested, at which he scratched his head thoughtfully for a few seconds.

"Oh, yes! Possibly! Probably!" and he prescribed a course of antibiotics. Again, no blood test, no confirmation, but by the grace of Allah, the medicine put her on the long and slow road to recovery.

⸙

Having no control over the kitchen doors, nor the front doors that were usually left open for the gudaam men, meant I had no control over the children's comings and goings. But if it worried me, they were in heaven and revelled in the freedom to roam outside. Sometimes, they would tell me when they were going, when they needed money to buy school stationary or something to eat, but more often they would simply go off and be back in their own good time. And they went together. That was an unspoken rule.

There was not a shopkeeper in our vicinity they did not know and who did not know them. *khilonay* (toy) *wallah*, *kitab* (book) *wallah*, *alloo cholay wallah* who made spicy chopped potatoes, radish, onions, and chickpeas, which he prepared in two coconut shell halves, cupping them together and shaking vigorously, blending all the flavours, and then serving it on a piece of paper, usually torn from a child's discarded school copy or backdated newspaper.

And then there was the *gol gappay wallah* with his scrumptious hollow, crispy-fried balls served with tamarind juice. *Shakar Qandi wallah* offered spice-covered chunks of soft sweet potatoes, again served on scraps of newspaper, which for me brought back memories of English fish and chips.

There were countless other vendors, and because the children made friends with them all, their innocent pleadings of

197

"Please baya!" would often win them a free portion, or a free second helping for all to share.

And it was not only food. Often, in the wholesale plastic market a plea of "Please, *bhaiya, sirf aik daina* (please brother, give us just one)," would pay off; and depending on what had caught their fancy, they would come home with anything from a miniature item of dolls' furniture, plastic whistle, cheap plastic ball, to a car with wobbly wheels that fell off almost as soon as they reached home. But they would be delighted, nonetheless.

Outside, there was always so much to see. In and around the bazaar, all manner of activities took place, humdrum happenings made interesting simply because they were so public. Men could sit on a chair by the roadside and have a shave or a haircut. They could have their ears cleaned, even dental treatment. And there was always a bustling medley of vehicles and pedestrians, weaving in and out of the narrow streets and alleyways.

Young boys and girls from the outskirts of the city or outlying villages would often pass through, herding a small flock of sheep or goats, coaxing them along with a stick. The children once saw a young girl herding some goats when she suddenly stood still as if waiting for someone. They looked on, curious to know what was happening. A few minutes later, before their very eyes, one of the goats gave birth to a kid, quickly followed by another one.

A Ramadhan to Remember

Ramadan 1982!

And it was summer, the most trying season of the year. Ramadan was always a joyous month. A month like no other! And the one time of the year when Muslims devote themselves to total obedience, submission, prayer, and spiritual rejuvenation, fasting from sunrise to sunset.

Fasting was never a problem for me. The first few days were usually difficult, but it soon became easier. We would wake up an hour or so before sunrise, and when the children were very small, we would prepare food with hushed voices so as not to wake them. Outside in the streets, a man would be doing his round, rousing everyone, beating, clanging, and shouting, *"Jago! Jago!* (Wake up! Wake up!)" and invariably the children would wake up and join us, which was actually good. At a very early age, they learnt what Ramadan and fasting was all about.

In our house, fasting usually began with a meal of parathas dipped in homemade yogurt. Ammi Ji's parathas were the best, and even on her little ungeethi she managed to cook them expertly. She would crush them, still piping hot, to make them flakier, and spread them with desi ghee to keep them soft. I envied her skill, and even when I managed to make them, mine could never compare to hers.

The first day of Ramadan, and I had fasted all day without any problem at all, but the moment I broke the fast I collapsed in a heap on the bed and could not get up again. I felt awful and completely drained of all strength and energy. I also had a very high fever. Since I was too weak to walk, Mustafa went to consult with the nearby doctor who asked him to describe my symptoms. His diagnosis was possible Malaria, one of the most common ailments, especially at that time of the year. So, Mustafa returned with quinine tablets.

I was supposed to get better, but I didn't. Still too weak to move or be moved, and with a recurring fever, Mustafa went back to the doctor to report that my symptoms were the same but worse. My temperature was higher. I felt weaker. I had pain in my abdomen and had lost my appetite.

This time, he brought home a course of antibiotics for pneumonia, and I was beginning to think we were on the same roulette wheel that Biba had been on when she was ill. I was the only one who suspected she had typhoid, but for some reason, maybe because my weakened state robbed me of the capacity to think clearly, I did not consider that possibility for myself. And because I had cramps in my lower abdomen like period pains, I guessed it might be something else altogether. So, I told Mustafa I needed to see a lady doctor urgently. Though weaker than before, with help from Mustafa and Bubbles, I made it down the stairs and across the courtyard to our Mini.

The pain and burning fever were due to a severe uterine infection, the doctor explained after examining me, and in typical doctor's scrawl wrote a prescription with instructions for administering the medication. "A course of penicillin injections and you'll be fine," she said.

Weaving in and out of traffic, honking other vehicles aside, Mustafa navigated the narrow, winding streets of the bazaar. He stopped immediately outside the pharmacy, a windowless, tube-lit room that served as shop-cum-clinic. I sat on a wooden bench while an assistant prepared to inject me with the antibiotic.

Glancing at the prescription, then at me, then the prescription again, he seemed to have difficulty deciphering the instructions, and when he asked me if I was supposed to take it as it was or diluted, I seriously began to doubt his competency. Alarm bells were ringing loud and clear, but I was too weak to challenge him.

A few moments of deliberation, and he injected the full, undiluted vial of Kanamycin, through the cotton shalwar I was wearing, into my thigh. My body's reaction was instant and spontaneous. A rush of intense heat spread through my leg, and as I left the premises, holding onto Mustafa, dazed and unsteady, I felt like a zombie. My entire body was now on fire, and I was beginning to hallucinate.

"Ring Mohammad," I said to Mustafa as he helped me into the car, "and tell him to be careful because the sky is about to fall down on us. I think it's the end of the world."

"Mummy, what's happened? You look terrible, and your eyes are completely bloodshot," Bubbles exclaimed when I arrived back home.

I looked in the mirror, which I should not have done because my face was like a monster from a horror movie. My head was now spinning wildly, and my mouth was so dry it kept sticking to the roof of my mouth. Even after drinking a full bottle of water, almost instantly my mouth became dry again. My mind, the small part that was still functioning properly, was telling me to drink as much water as I could to flush the medicine out of my body. So that is what I did.

That night, devotees in the mosques were praying, the sound of Quranic recitations resounding throughout the city, but my bemused, fever-stricken mind conjured the notion there were musicians in the rooms below.

"There are thieves in the house," I whispered to Mustafa. "They've broken into the gudaams, and they're singing and making music. You have to stop them."

"Accha! Accha! I'll check it out!" Mustafa replied, prudently not questioning, or disputing my hallucinations.

Over the next few days, I became progressively worse. Clearly, Kanamycin was not curing me. Quite the contrary! Could the lady doctor's diagnosis be wrong, everyone began to question because whatever ailment I was suffering from had an even firmer grip on my body? How or why or when I do not know, but it was finally decided that I should have a blood test at a proper diagnostic clinic. The results were overwhelmingly positive for typhoid. Untreated for so long, the Salmonella typhi count was alarmingly high.

At last, the right treatment could begin, a course of Chloramphenicol tablets. But I was now so weak I could not speak and could barely open my mouth to swallow the tablets or sip the thin porridge that Bubbles made for me. I was in a very dark place. I thought I was going to die and was losing the will to live anyway.

One evening, while I was lying on my bed, the children were watching Shogun, a Japanese-based film series starring Richard Chamberlain, and I remember, in my weakened state, listening to the violent dialogue and feeling terrified. Even more frightening, I saw myself falling into a dark, endless abyss. A moment of absolute terror! And in that dark, delirious, swoon-like state, I desperately fought to get out. I wanted to run far away to somewhere peaceful and safe. Regaining my senses, I silently prayed. "Allah, please help me. Please take me from this world."

Moments later, Tommy, who still drank milk from a feeder, wriggled onto the bed and lay down beside me, one small arm holding his bottle in the air to allow the milk to flow freely, the other resting across my tummy. He was the quiet, shy one of the family, but his small, soft hand, stretching across to hold onto me, said more than any words could ever express.

And then little Noori quietly climbed onto the bed the other side of me. Gently stroking my face with her tiny hand, she said, "I love you mummy. You are so beautiful."

One moment, I was praying for death. The next, I was pleading with Allah to help me. I could not die and leave my lovely children behind. Bless them! They brought me back from the brink of despair that awful day.

***

It took me a very long time to recover. It was the only time in my life that I lost so much weight. I could have been knocked down with a feather! I needed time to heal, both physically and mentally; and more importantly, I needed time to reflect.

The children were happy. They had settled down and this House of Doors was unquestionably their home. The older ones said the daily prayers, and could read the Holy Quran, which was the reason I came to Pakistan. So why was I not happy?

The answer? I had no social life, and no real friends. The children went to school or college, and they had both. I still struggled with Urdu, but they could speak it fluently, read and write it, too. But these were all excuses, I reprimanded myself. The problem must be with me.

We are not angels, but simple human beings with feelings, failings, and aspirations. If it had not been for my faith and my children, I might have drowned in my own sorrow. Taking care of the children kept me going, although there were times I could not shake off the guilt that on so many levels I was failing them. I half-resigned myself to the fact that what I desired for them and myself was not meant to be. But not completely. The desire kept creeping back.

Life is tough. That is the way it is, and the way God tests us to make us better and stronger. If you have ever watched an artisan at work, you might see him take a chunk of wood or marble and visualise something beautiful in it. He then picks up his tools and sets to work, hacking, hammering, scraping, and chiselling it into shape. He files and polishes it until it is the beautiful, perfect object he envisaged.

If the piece of wood or marble had a voice it would cry out, "Stop! It hurts. Why are you doing this to me?" And the artisan would answer, "It is the only way to make you into something beautiful." The wood or the marble would then thank him for all the time and trouble he was taking to make it into something worth cherishing.

And that is how and why God puts us through trials and tribulations – to perfect us and make us the way He wants us to be. As a Muslim, I believe that death is not the end, but the beginning of the Life Hereafter. And what we receive in that life depends on how firm our faith is, our words and deeds, and how well we follow His commands. Ultimately, it depends on His mercy.

Submission

Fast-forwarding several years!

The thirteen years came and went, something I should never have believed in, or even thought about. Superstition belongs in the domain of paganism, not religion, and most definitely not in Islam. So, once again I had to reprimand myself.

For years, too many years I am ashamed to admit, Mustafa followed a so-called *peer sahib*, or spiritual guide called Baba Ji, and because he believed in him, I did, too. Before making any decision, from the children's education to home or monetary affairs, Mustafa would consult Baba Ji. But over time, I began to suspect that Baba Ji had neither the spiritual acumen nor psychic power he professed. And sometimes, he would do things that I believed to be contrary to his own preaching.

He often asked for money. He advised us to live simply, but when his son was married, it was not only a very lavish, insalubrious affair, no expenses spared, in many ways I thought it was vulgar, unnecessary, and insensitive.

Their neighbour had died the night before the marriage, but still there were firecrackers, a cacophonous band dressed in uniform, and several specially hired dancers with *ghunghroo*, their long, brightly coloured skirts twirling, rupee notes being showered like confetti over their heads as they danced to the rhythm of the blaring trumpets and deafening drums. And that is when decided I would no longer follow him.

There are, it saddens me to say, countless fake peers who fool innocent people into believing they have the power to grant them children, bring about a change in financial status, produce suitable proposals for their daughters, cure all manner of illnesses, and more.

The worst of them are tricksters, thieves, blackmailers, rapists, smugglers, purveyors of drugs and black magic potions designed to turn enemies into friends or vice versa, create a serious rift between husband and wife, or even make someone ill. They prey on the illiterate, weak and vulnerable and get rich by them. And they do it all in the name of religion.

Many of the devotees are not free from blame, either. Generally illiterate, though not by choice but by the purposeful design of the feudal lords who rule over them, they blindly worship these self-acclaimed saints, a sin tantamount to *shirk*, ascribing gods or partners besides Allah. While He forgives all manner of sins, *shirk* is the one sin He says He will not forgive.

Our faith requires that we attribute ultimate power to God. If a medicine cures us, it is because it is His will. If we work hard for an exam and do well, it is because God wills it. Pride on the other hand leads us to believe achievement is due to our own effort alone.

Qarun, known as Korah in the Bible, was Pride personified. An Israelite who lived at the time of Musa (Moses), he became one of Pharaoh's chief advisors. By dint of his God-given talents, Qarun had amassed enormous wealth and power, and had so many chests full of treasures that the keys to unlock them were too heavy for any one man to lift. He was often seen dragging the hefty chain of keys along the ground, his head proudly held high, and his long robes trailing behind him.

Musa advised Qarun to make better use of his wealth by helping those less fortunate. "Your worldly gains," Musa told him, "are all due to God's blessings, so share it with those in need."

Qarun was so greedy and miserly; nothing could ever persuade him to part with his treasures. His wealth had nothing to do with God, he argued. It was the result of his own ingenuity and hard work. And so, because of his pride, ingratitude and miserliness, God caused the ground to open beneath him, and it swallowed him up, along with his home and all his treasures.

By my own admission, faith is not believing in God when things are going your way, nor when you see incredible things happen. Faith is to believe when the going is tough, when you cannot see the light at the end of the tunnel, yet you are certain it is there. But there was one thing still missing, and it was the reason for my negativity and discontent. It was submission. *Total submission!*

Like a eureka moment, I had finally found the flaw in my faith. God knew everything about me, where and how I was living, all the struggles, the joyous times, too. So, what was there to be miserable or complain about? And in that moment of spiritual awakening, I bowed my head and prayed, a prayer that sprang from the very depths of my soul.

"Oh Allah! If this is where you want me to live for the rest of my days. If I die here, and my body is taken from this house, I am content, because I know You are watching over me, and only You know what is best for me."

With both hands, I then took the desires from my heart and laid them before Him. A blissful moment of total, unconditional surrender, and submission! And that is the meaning, the essence of Islam; to submit to the will of God. And when you attain that perfection, you can aspire to being a Momin, a true Muslim. And that is when Allah rewards you in ways you could never, ever imagine.

However, it is one thing to attain perfection in faith, or near perfection since perfection is essentially unattainable, but to hold onto it and prevent it from slipping away is thereafter a perpetual struggle because the devil, ever faithful to his promise to corrupt mankind, works overtime to pull us down and make us fail.

Ever mindful, I remind myself to tread ever so softly in this life's journey; not to avoid leaving footprints behind, but to avoid trampling others and causing them harm. Heart and soul looking upward to Heaven, head bowed in submission and humility, and eyes focussed on the road ahead to see where I am going!

<hr />

Barely two weeks later, Mustafa came home from the market to tell us the exciting news that a group of businessmen in the market wanted to buy our house. The party was so keen, they were willing to put down a deposit immediately. It was unbelievable.

Words cannot describe how we all felt. Not long ago, I had happily resigned myself to life in this house, and now Allah was offering me the escape that over the years I had shed many tears yearning for. But that is the miracle of total submission. The following then became my daily prayer:

"O Lord! I am nothing but what You have made me. I have nothing but what You have given me. Accept my humble thanks for Your countless blessings and pardon me for my countless sins. You alone do we worship. You alone do we ask for help, for only You have the power to hear our prayers and answer them.

"Only You have the power to provide for us, protect us, guide us, and pardon us. Only You have the power to make things happen. Guide me, that I may earn Your pleasure, never Your displeasure, and grant me a place in al-Firdaus, ameen."

About a month later, I said farewell to the house I had lived in for eighteen years and moved to pastures green outside the walled city. Times had changed and so had women's fashion, so when we moved, I left the burka behind and wore a *chaddar*, a large shawl, instead.

Bubbles ultimately became a doctor, Beenish, too. Jimmy went to England for business studies, but not before graduating with a bachelor's degree, for which I did most of the work, reading course books he found boring and making notes for him.

Desi was obsessed with anything mechanical and electrical and had collected so much cable wire we used to tease him that he must be planning to join it all together to reach the moon. Not surprisingly, he became an engineer. Tommy did, too. Biba and Noori, both averse to science subjects, attained art degrees, their main subject being psychology.

House on the Hill Revisited

Our journey had not ended. Almost twenty three years after first setting foot in Pakistan, I was flying to England for the very first time. Biba, now married and living in the coastal town of Poole in Dorset, was expecting her first baby and wanted me to be there for the birth.

Could I come, she had asked, and there was no hesitation from either of us. Noori would go with me and Mustafa would stay behind with Beenish and Tommy, the two other chidren still living with us. Jimmy and Desi were already in England, and Bubbles was married and working in a local hospital in Lahore.

Just two days before my flight, Ammi Ji had a stroke and was rushed to hospital where she underwent emergency surgery to remove a clot from the brain. I went to see her, but the nurses refused to let me inside the ward.

"I'm flying to London early tomorrow morning. I *have* to see her before I go." I insisted. So, reluctantly they allowed me in.

I shall never forget that ward. The lights were purposely dim, and I could just make out row upon row of beds occupied by post operative patients, their heads bandaged, bodies motionless. And I remember thinking it was like a waiting room for death.

Ammi Ji was in the bed closest to the door. I spoke to her, but she did not respond. Her eyes closed, she was deeply asleep, probably still sedated after the major operation she had undergone. Gently, I touched her feet and said a silent prayer, promising that on my return I would take care of her, for I did not think she would fully recover. It was more likely she would be paralysed, but hopefully, only partially.

Jimmy met us at Heathrow. He now worked in the government patent department, had his own small terrace house and a Honda hatchback he was extremely proud of. Driving along the motorway was like going back to the future, to an England that partly resembled the one I had left over two decades ago, but at the same time was strangely new.

Motorways criss-crossing the land, massive supermarkets and warehouses, old houses demolished and replaced by modern edifices. I even saw Pakistani women walking along the high streets, wearing dupattas, and shalwar kameez beneath their heavy overcoats. There were halal shops, and every district had its own mosque, a converted house usually, but a mosque all the same. Once, I passed by a church that had been converted into a mosque. How times had changed!

It was soon after we arrived at Biba's home that we learned of Ammi Ji's death. She died early the same morning we left, while we were in the air. The peculiar juxtaposition of life and death! I had come for the birth of Biba's baby, only to be greeted with the news of Ammi Ji's death.

I was now more anxious than ever to find my family. Before leaving for England, I had asked Mohammad to trace their whereabouts so I could meet them if possible, but for many days there was no news from him. And then, about two weeks after my arrival, a very excited Mohammad rang me to say he had found my youngest sister, and asked if I would like to meet her.

"Of course," I replied. "Where does she live? And what about my parents? Where are they?"

There was a pause, and then the news I was totally unprepared for. "I'm sorry, but they are both dead. Your mum died first of a stroke, and your dad died a few years later. I think he had cancer."

Now choked with emotion, I told Mohammad I would ring him later, and put the phone back on its cradle. It was a lot to take in. Ammi Ji's death when I felt sure she would live, and now to learn that my parents were gone, too. I never imagined when I left them that I would not see them again. But that's what we so often do. Take people, parents especially, for granted.

Dark clouds eventually waft away and sunshine fills the sky once more. I met one of my brothers and all three sisters. The one whose clothes I borrowed without asking, the one who made the mince pies every Christmas, and the youngest and the prettiest of us all. There was a moment of disorientation when I saw them, and then, like a flash of light, instant recognition; and all the years in between seemed to dissipate. It was heart-warming to see them, even though a barrier still divided us. Their homes were in England. Mine was in Pakistan.

***

We went to our home that was, the House on the Hill, and gave Ruth the surprise of her life. She invited us to stay overnight, but we couldn't. Biba was nearing her due date and needed me. After all, that was why I was there.

Three weeks after the safe arrival of Biba's daughter, Noori and I returned to Pakistan. It had been an incredibly uplifting journey. We had met my family, my dear friend Ruth, and spent many precious hours with Jimmy and Desi, who lived together.

Desi was studying computer science in university, and working part time in a fish and chip shop to help cover living expenses, enjoying the perk of a free meal, which was good for filling the stomach but not for the waistline, as evident from Desi's rather rotund figure.

My world had suddenly become wider and brighter. In Pakistan, I had a home in greener pastures with a garden of flowers, even a banana tree. I had time to reflect, to appreciate how Allah had taken care of us all the years we lived inside the walled city. How He had fulfilled my foremost desire, that my children should grow up as Muslims. Without the support of Mustafa's family, without the aunt, may Allah bless and reward her, who taught them how to read the Holy Quran, I could never have achieved that goal.

For every story told, there are hundreds untold. For words and feelings expressed, countless remain unspoken, hidden in the deepest recesses of the mind or heart or soul. Likewise, this has been only a glimpse into my life in Lahore. No saris or servants galore, but a life enriched by my children and those precious moments of spiritual awakening, the quiet reveries over the years having hopefully enlightened me and broadened my horizons.

One thing I have observed is the propensity of man (woman too, of course) to be careless and complacent. And to be blind! He wears blinkers or rose-tinted glasses and channels his energy into improving his fiscal and social status in life to the detriment of his soul. Aware, or perhaps unaware, that the countdown from birth to the end of life has begun, he neglects those altruistic acts of empathy, kindness, and compassion, as well as worship and prayer, the vital prerequisites for a passport to Paradise. Hence my poem, Countdown.

Countdown

At break of dawn, a baby is born.
His little chest heaves to take its first sweet
breath.
His tiny heart leaps joyfully like a frolicking
lamb
Inebriated with the sweet-scented breeze
And thrilling miracle of spring.
And like warm waters, kissing and
embracing sun-blessed shores,
From his small heart, the vibrant flow of
life
Surges within his gentle form
As he sleeps in innocent bliss,
Oblivious that with the steady pounding
of his heart
The countdown has begun.

The babe becomes a man.
King of all the land, and Lord of his own
universe,
He spends his carefree days pursuing
fruitless pleasures,
Craving endless treasures and accruing
countless sins.
He sees the far horizons, hears the
distant hum,
But not the warning drumbeats deep
within.

Summer ends. The old man bends,
Like a weakened willow burdened with too
many bows,
Involuntarily submitting to the harsh will
of the wind.

Defiantly, the heart throbs on,
Then, faltering, it skips a beat,
But the pounding, ever loud and strong,
Like the clashing of a mighty gong,
Reiterates its urgent song.
The countdown has begun.

Too late! Time spent has gone and will not
come again.
What's past and done cannot be done again.
The heartbeat stops. The countdown ends.
No time, no chance to make amends.

About the Author

Once a devout Christian, Lillian Greene's life changed dramatically when she encountered two Muslims at a church meeting and was intrigued by their religious beliefs. Soon after, she embraced Islam and spent most of her adult life in Pakistan, bringing up an ever-growing family and struggling to adapt to a new way of life. This book is a brief but true account of that journey.

Printed in the United States
by Baker & Taylor Publisher Services